MUSIC AND THE CHILD
EXPERIENCES OF A PIANO TEACHER

Erna Czövek

MUSIC AND THE CHILD

EXPERIENCES OF A PIANO TEACHER

Corvina Kiadó

Title of the original: Emberközpontú zenetanítás
Zeneműkiadó Budapest, 1975
Translated by Godfrey Offord
Design by Zsuzsa László
© Erna Czövek, 1975, 1979
ISBN 963 13 0700 X
Printed in Hungary, 1979
Franklin Printing House, Budapest

CONTENTS

I PREFACE   7

II MUSIC   11
   1 Man and artistic education   11
   2 The laws of music   14
   3 Music—its content and form   19

III THE CHILD   24
   1 Musical instruction and child mentality   24
   2 Teaching beginners   29

IV PSYCHOLOGICAL REQUIREMENTS   37
   1 The revision of piano teaching methods   37
   2 Types of ability   38
   3 The analysis of talent   39
   4 Imagination   46

V THE ETHICAL SIDE OF MUSIC TEACHING   48
   1 Teaching and the human aspect   48
   2 Inflexible music teaching   50
   3 The formation of a work ethic   53

VI THE QUESTION OF "STYLE"   56
   1 Definition of terms   56
   2 Stylistic constraint, stylistic confusion   58
   3 Teaching the various styles   58
   4 Teachers, performers and style   63

VII TECHNIQUE 66
    1 Its place in piano teaching 66
    2 The balance of the body 67
    3 The role of the fingers 69
    4 Ways of striking the keys 73
    5 Fingering 74
    6 The teacher's physical involvement 75

VIII PROFESSIONAL TRAINING AND MASS EDUCATION 76
    1 The diversity of music 76
    2 Reform and revolution 77
    3 Making a choice 80
    4 Streaming 81
    5 Auxiliary subjects 83

I PREFACE

Music teaching as a creative activity

"Deep within us exists the creative force that is able to create that which must be, and it will not grant us rest or repose until one way or another, without or within us, it has been able to manifest itself."

Goethe

The instinct to create

Two main forces motivate every living creature: the instinct for personal survival and the instinct to preserve the species.

All behaviour of living creatures can be traced back to these two instincts. The first determines all behaviour of creatures both as a group and individually, provided its vital influence is not diminished through some psychological disorder. The second is none other than the survival instinct's own kind of self-preservation; for living creatures take care to ensure that they will go on living after their physical death, transmitting what can be salvaged from their mortal remains to their successors. In animals, the instinct to preserve the species is a force of such power that, at times, it will take precedence over the instinct for self-preservation. Man sublimates this instinct, as he is apt to do with all his instincts; the more gifted he is, the greater the extent to which he does so. What is art if not the most cultured and most splendid manifestation of the instinct to preserve the species?

Creative teaching

Man lives on not only in his children but in his creations too. The further away he gets from primeval nature, the more important to him will be the sense of "immortality", the hold on life which finds expression in creation. This is not vanity, it is instinct.

Man is capable of being just as biassed and conceited about his creations as about his children, and yet, at the same time, just as attentively observant of their development and fate. (Of course, some parents may be modest and relatively unbiased, just as they can be neglectful and unconscientious too.) The teacher should realize that his teaching and all his pedagogical activity is creation. This is how he should interpret his vocation, and he should respect it as an instinct striving for immortality. His sphere of influence covers pupil, environment and the surrounding culture, and so he is responsible both to his pupils and, more importantly, to himself. The way he deals with this creative instinct—at times the strongest instinct of all—depends not only on his talent but also on his freedom of will.

Creative teaching is instruction in independent activity

The teacher creates by arousing in his pupils that particular instinct which finds sublimation in art; in other words, he forms their musical taste and activates their musical needs in such a way that his pupils progress on their own terms, developing their own abilities.

The creative instinct as the factor determining the quality of life

In the real sense, the aim of life is not determined by each individual but by some higher idea in whose service he may enlist. Either this aim corresponds to the creative needs of the person concerned or it does not. If the individual finds an idea that is able to determine the aim of his life for at least a considerable period of time, he will not feel his life to be without direction, and his spiritual equilibrium will be largely in order. His creative needs will also be satisfied. Such cases, however, are rare and fortunate and the person does not have to exert any fundamental influence through his own will. Conversely, if the chosen aim in life does not correspond to the person's creative type, he may feel his life to be wasted. Apart from some form of communal commitment, however, a person can hold on to a particular idea that he regards as his aim in life; he might be a world-famous artist, for instance, or save and enrich someone else's life. Nevertheless aims such as these are usually of limited duration, and their significance lies not so much in the aim itself as in the activity undertaken in the interests of the aim.

In the last analysis, true aims in life alter in the course of man's social development, and the individual cannot permanently be attached to one single aim.

The teacher, whose vocation involves keeping foremost in mind the well-being of people, should turn his attention to the quality of young people's lives. (This does not, of course, prevent the young people from accurately determining an aim in life, on the contrary, it positively helps.)

The teacher's work should assist the pupil to instruct himself. This is the pedagogy of life. One does not have to be a teacher by vocation or even simply by profession to perceive this. We all educate ourselves, and the only achievements that have real value are those we accomplish through our own efforts. A teacher, drawing on his teaching ability and his general experiences, can help a pupil find his own subject for self-instruction. The teacher can also find out the pupil's own inclinations and help develop these too. A gifted teacher may go further still and help the pupil to the extent that the pupil need not rely solely on the teacher's directions but, indeed, discover some of these for himself. It is not only the teacher who educates people; everyone educates himself and those around him. The teacher can sometimes do a lot of good and, occasionally, a lot of harm. Teaching is therefore a serious creative vocation.

The teacher's role in music appreciation

With luck, the quality of one's life is determined by one's vocation. In most cases, however, our lives are not defined by a vocation and we do the bulk of our everyday work from a sense of duty or from sheer necessity. In these cases we do not feel the sense of creation in the execution of our main activity; and, as a result, we no longer seek it in our work or we bottle it up, or even look for it elsewhere. The frustration of the creative urge can easily lead to catastrophic results which is why one of the teacher's most important tasks is to help the pupil set himself on the right course which will, in turn, help determine the quality of his life, even if he lacks the necessary talent for it to become a vocation.

Directed recreation and love of art can fill this gap, which is why we must pay as much attention to these things as we do to the development of our chosen careers, or, in more fortunate cases, our vocations.

This is where music teaching, which provides one with a lifetime's delight, links up with teaching generally; and this in essence is the meaning and the merit of aesthetic education. With artistic instruction and creative music teaching we are in many cases striving to develop vocational awareness, but in the majority of cases we are trying to fashion that activity which will enrich life. If teaching is understood in this way then it is not the pupil's "talent" that is decisive, but the extent to which we are able to accomplish the above "creatively", that is, in such a way that our instruction has effect on the pupil's independent activity. We achieve little on the pupil's behalf if year by year we make him learn a few pieces in which his performance conforms to our conception; in other words forcing the result from him "by rote". The creative teaching method is to educate the pupil's ear to apprehend the musical thought through his own conception. This means educating musically the pupil through his piano pieces in such a way that his performance is based on his own conception and not the teacher's. This can be achieved to a greater or lesser extent with every pupil. Musical taste and imagination develop gradually, not as pieces are worked up to greater and greater perfection, but as the construction and shaping of the piece is gradually perceived.

II MUSIC

1 Man and artistic education

"Artistic education is not an aim in itself"

We do not need to concern ourselves with the arts in order to understand them better, nor in order to "switch off" after a day's work. If that were the case, it would justify the educator's question: art—or sport?

In principle—at a higher, official level—everyone agrees that artistic education is necessary, but the question, why is it necessary—is generally unsatisfactory, and is either misleading, or, at best, illuminates one or two details. Music specialists do not justify artistic education.

The specialists working in the different branches of music—composers, performers, or those in musicological fields—treat music teaching at the lower level, at best as a side issue. Occasionally one or two first-class composers or performers bring themselves to write down their pedagogical experiences, and although these works are instructive and thought-provoking, they do not generally go into great depth on the subject of the psychological aspect of music teaching. Music teachers tend to be subjective when they write about teaching, and dwell on matters of detail; while if psychologists deal with music teaching, their treatment of instrumental teaching is at best peripheral.

The effect of the arts on the human mind is exceptionally complex, and for this reason even those who themselves favour the arts and believe in artistic education often lose their bearings and despite good intentions fail to give a clear picture of their subject.

In their own sphere the arts differ greatly from each other, but their common features are their most fundamental ones. *They have in common that they are a sublime, more elevated psychic mirror of life.* The essence of art, unquestionably the most elevated manifestation of human evolution is man's *conscious, rational ability to plan*. If he develops this ability throughout his life, through his positive inclinations, the education he receives, and later through self-education, he will progress to ever higher levels on the road to the human ideal. If, however, he turns his endeavours towards inferior regions, he will sink mentally ever lower as life passes. It is immaterial whether this sinking occurs under the influence of difficult living conditions, or whether the downward drop comes as a result of the mental faculties succumbing to material possibilities. In both cases *the human mind is being under-exploited* and instincts are not being raised to a higher level.

Artistic education can produce equilibrium here, and therein lies its significance. *Its aim, therefore, is to raise primitive human instincts to a high level.*

The practice of art cannot be equated with recreation (by recreation I mean pleasantly languid mental relaxation), since the mind does not cease its activity while art is performed or enjoyed. Art is not restful like recreation, as we are not passive participants. We have to pay attention, and this demands a certain mental exertion. If this is missing, then we are not taking part in art but simply enjoying ourselves. If dealing with the arts in addition to everyday work is refreshing, this is not the result of relaxed mental activity, but of the mind's active spiritual identification with art.

To understand this, one should not erect too rigid a dividing wall between the passive and active enjoyment of art. In fact there is no such thing as the passive enjoyment of art. He whose spirit does not participate in art as it manifests itself is not really enjoying the work.

As I have said, the essence of art is man's conscious rational planning ability. The creation of a work of art is therefore the methodical shaping of material. The work itself is the material already shaped. In terms of mental participation the true enjoyer of art, when immersing himself in the work, and, if sufficiently talented, is able to form a critical judgement of the work and may be prevented from enjoying it if the solution offered is poor. His joy—if he is really immersed in the work—comes very close to the lofty satisfaction felt by its creator. Intensive involvement with art is the noblest vindication of human feelings.

But is it clear to educators in the arts just how the arts achieve this?

The spectrum of pedagogical activity is extremely broad. To a certain extent everyone, from the lecturer in the local house of culture to Neuhaus*, is a music teacher. Everyone—the layman, the dilettante—can get usefully involved in patronage or even propaganda of the arts without any expert knowledge. I have known more than one music enthusiast whose interest in music was aroused by a couple of romantic biographies, and who, after listening to numerous second-rate efforts, came to appreciate first rate performances of masterpieces, and turned from a spontaneous enthusiast into a connoisseur and a true participant in the musical human ideal. To state this is not perfectionism, but the result of genuinely exercised critical faculties. If we trust to chance or obscure the comprehensible facts, we shall not arrive at the human, formative meaning of art. And if we look on art merely as recreation or escapism, how will we understand the difference between Shakespeare and trashy novels, Rembrandt and daubers, Bach and pop music?

---

*H. G. Neuhaus, Soviet music teacher, also taught Richter. His main work on music teaching is *The Art of Piano Playing*.

As there are so few music teachers who have not unwillingly turned from art to teaching we must unfortunately rely on semi-professionals (of varying merit) who have taken to cultural propagation not out of knowledge but out of goodwill.

However, well-intentioned but unqualified mass education cannot aspire to the ranks of informed artistic teaching, and is certainly no substitute for it. It is not enough for the teacher of the arts to have a feeling for art and teaching; he must be knowledgeable too. First and foremost he must be able to recognize and follow the essence of a work: the consciously planned combinative work of the artist, i.e., the way the work has been formed. And it is not for the sake of explaining the form of the work under study to the pupil that he must be able to follow this process. Whether a work is a rondo or a fugue or in sonata form can be worked out and decided without getting any nearer the way the work is built up. What grips us in art is the creative artist's form giving power, by means of which he conceives the whole work as an entity and fits it together logically from the sequence of details. The superbly fashioned totality of a Gothic church, a combination of the rich ornamentation of countless magnificent figures. A picture by Mihály Munkácsy, where the perfection of the whole composition entrances us to such a degree because the individual figures and their all-expressive features together fashion its unity. Finally, a Beethoven sonata or Bartók's music in the way the whole is built up out of the movements, and the movements take their shape from the interplay of the motives without the slightest break. The macrocosm and microcosm lie hidden in all true art. The work's totality consists in the interplay of motives and their logical interconnection.

It is the primary task of music teaching to get this across. The artist creates the work and the appreciative audience follows in the tracks of the creation—through the medium of the performer. The intervention of the performer, however, does not rescue the listener from active participation—indeed, it places still greater responsibility upon him: now he must keep track of the interpreter's truth as well as that of the creator. Anyone who simply rushes through exhibitions, the Forum Romanum or even a performance of Beethoven's symphonies, and feels he has had a good time—who found not emotion but merely escapism—has not enriched his mind by what he has seen or heard. And given that he has not done much for his health either after the day's physical or mental exercise, he would have done better to have done some sport. To appreciate the essence he would need an art-master or music teacher to teach him to see or hear.

So what is music we should identify with?

2 The laws of music

Music teaching usually divides musical sounds into two groups to understand and assess them:

A) rhythm—beat: the relationship of divisions in time and their dynamic execution.

B) melody—harmony: the relationship of divisions according to pitch and the way they take effect in the movement and grouping of sound.

A) The basis of the *first group* is the time, or the beat, indicated in traditional music by the time-signature.

In this group the psychological momentum is the striving of basically undirected, ineluctable primeval man towards order and civilization. With primitive races, the regular pulse was ensured by the percussion instruments, while for the civilized it has been the monotonous rhythm of dance music—reinforced perhaps by clapping in folk dancing—followed by jazz and most recently the developed percussion techniques of pop music. A rhythmic pulse, however, has to survive even in the demands of the most complex musical taste; and something that does not exhibit traces of man's striving for regularity cannot be called music. (Even if it is not in the form of the regular pulse that prevailed in the classical period.) If there is nothing to arouse a sense of regularity, then one of music's elements—a temporal reference-point, disappears. This element meets our mental requirements, not through its rhythmic but through its imposition of order, as well as being a prerequisite of the creation of form. If there is no organized rhythmic pulse, then the possibility of shaping the music and making cross-references disappears, and the form loses its meaning. There is no meaningful music without formal relationships.

Here is a clear practical example of the interdependence of rhythm, beat and form. One of the tests in musical examinations is clapping back a rhythm. The examiner claps out a rhythm which the candidate has to clap back. The correct way of doing this is when the examiner is conscious of a formal pattern to the rhythm, e.g.

If his clapping is clear in the sense that the binary form can be followed, then it will be correctly repeated, and possible minor discrepancies will not matter, e.g.

or some other variant. But if the examiner claps with no sense of form, the pupil will not be able to follow the rhythm; he will muddle it, and may add or leave bits out. Of course the pupil who has no sense of form will not understand the correct example either. He will be said to have no sense of rhythm. Rhythm can only exist when there is a steady beat for it to relate to, and a sense of form. A rhythm such as: ♫ for instance, cannot be felt. ♫♩ | or ♫♩|♩ are the smallest forms that can be grasped. If we turn our attention to a sensitivity to order, and a sense of form, then a sense of rhythm—the basis of all musical training—can be developed in the highest degree. This kind of development of a sense of rhythm will not be advanced by the use of rhythmically spoken syllables—a singularly primitive and harmful educational concept—first because it directs attention towards syllable and not rhythm, and secondly, because it identifies high and low vowel sounds with short and long.

Only movements, or sounds combined with movements—tapping and perhaps clapping or singing—are suitable for rhythmic exercises. Tapping as a form of beating is the most suitable as it can combine sound with an extremely simple movement.

Dividing up rhythm meaningfully can solve another constantly recurring problem.

It is a well-known peculiarity of children to believe that the faster their fingers move, the better they are playing. As they have no other standard, this is understandable. But if from the outset their attention is drawn to the fact that music has a meaningful expressive content and form, they will be willing to control this. In time they will learn music's "language", and when that has happened they will not go galloping senselessly away however fast they can play the piece.

The question now is how to get across the rhythmic span, the rhythm itself and its framework, the beat.

It is commonly believed that this is achieved by means of the strong beats.

In this connection we need to examine the essence of rhythm more closely.

True rhythmic playing is not characterized by metronome-like regularity. If we look at the playing of the great masters of rhythm—including the good jazz musicians—we realize that the rhythmically important notes are not played with mathematical exactness (nor indeed do the melodically sensitive ones)—they come *later,* to a more or less noticeable extent. Today this is usually called agogics. In talking of beating time, I referred to the connection between the two parts of a binary phrase. This, too, can only be expressed by agogics and not by accentuation!

This can best be felt in the important, weighty bass notes and in those that stand out melodically. It is even valid for dance-music. Only the military band plays with metronome-like precision, emphasizing the beats with cymbals and drums. Rhythm compelled to follow such relentlessly strict time is only useful for marching. Generally speaking it is *not* accent that marks time; a rhythmic dictation where the teacher accents all the downbeats is very primitive. There are, of course, as we have already learnt, downbeats and upbeats, which create rhythmic variety by their interplay with syncopated or dotted rhythms. But only in certain cases may a beat be marked by a *dynamic* accent. The way the rhythm is played will be determined by the music's form and its structural divisions; this cannot be written down as a rule and learnt, it is part of the art of performing; there are as many interpretations as there are musical thoughts. The difference between the playing of musical and unmusical pupils becomes apparent chiefly in the extent to which they are able to execute these subtle distinctions, which cannot be taught, but can be brought to the pupil's notice by good music teaching.

B) The laws of the *second group* are much more complicated than those of the first; it is no accident that this group became part of musical creation at a much later stage. Melody is a far more refined emotional sublimation than rhythm which still carries much of its primitive ancestry within it: expression in melody, while equally the manifestation of an instinct in origin, presupposes a higher cultural level and is composed of more constituents. We have all heard of singing dogs, and marvelled at bird-song; such sounds may be music-like, as a result of their regular vibration, but not even the sweetest bird-song or the musical barking can be music, for it does not fulfil music's criteria.

a) In examining pitch, let us first consider *the categories of the musical ear*.

From the point of view of judging pitch, there exists on the one hand *perfect* and *relative* pitch, by which the pitch of notes is registered, and on the other a sensitivity to sound, *a sense of tone colour*.

In both these cases the ear's ability can be developed to a greater or lesser extent, and for this reason a thorough knowledge of aural training methods are necessary.

Public opinion sets great store by perfect pitch. It is very impressive if someone can recognize any note by its pitch with absolute certainty. The reliability of perfect pitch depends on the person's ability to memorize certain notes and recall them. It is relatively easy to develop it up to a point in relation to one's own instrument or voice. Most violinists, for instance, hear the A above middle C with perfect certainty, as a result of starting their tuning with it every day. A pianist can develop a similar capacity by repeating the same note at different times of the day before he has had a chance to relate it to others. This limited form of perfect pitch centred on one note can be worked up in a sol-fa group, by beginning the singing with the same note every time, for example. Singers and wind-players can acquire it with the aid of their throat and blowing muscles. Perfect pitch that is totally reliable and extends to every note is more likely to appear in early childhood and is virtually inherited by musicians' children.

For instrumental players, perfect pitch has no special significance; it can greatly facilitate the work of conductors, choirmasters and singing teachers, making their correction of intonation reliable—and greatly impressing the members of the orchestra—but musically it is not really an advantage. Indeed, in recognizing and judging intervals it is often more of a hindrance than a help (as Martienssen* has pointed out). A musician who has grown accustomed to recognizing sounds on their own without comparing them to others is generally less apt to attend to the relationship of one note to the other. The attention of a musician with perfect pitch centres primarily on the individual note, though attention to the interrelationship of notes is as important for him as it is for the person without perfect pitch. Recognizing intervals and the connection between notes, i.e. the faculty of relative pitch, is much more important for a musician. The two sorts of pitch are often compared with each other, with perfect pitch generally being the more highly respected. Yet there are music teachers who affirm that reliable relative pitch is of greater value. In my opinion, however, a comparison of the two is of little value as the possession of either is no guarantee that someone is a good musician. Relative pitch laboriously acquired at sol-fa and theory lessons and a sure recognition of intervals or even classical harmonies are not enough to enable someone to understand the emotional content of music or the way that "the piece has been formed". A sense of relative pitch is nothing other than a technical orientation and comprehension, within general musical culture.

As we shall see below in the chapter on technique, it is not a good thing for technical training as a separate activity to occupy too large a place in musical studies, for the role of technique is simply to be of service to artistic execution. It is its prerequisite. We all know a good ear is not an end in itself, but few people realize that its training is only necessary insofar as the individual pupil's development demands it. Prestabilized harmony (to be explained in the next chapter) along with imagination, ear and a certain amount of keyboard facility, ideally renders technical practice for its own sake virtually superfluous. The same goes for general ear training. For those who can execute the musical concept which they have in their ear, ear training for its own sake is hardly necessary. Of course not all children are equally talented and some may require more help than others who are more gifted. The ultimate object of teaching is to bring the lesser endowed pupils as near as possible to the capability of the talented. Here, of course, certain well worked-out methods can help, and

---

*K. A. Martienssen followed Edwin Fischer as departmental head at the Deutsche Hochschule der Musik in Berlin. His main work is *Schöpferischer Klavierunterricht*.

this is where the greatest danger arises, one that has not spared even modern teaching practice. Well worked-out methods, which have undoubtedly evolved on the basis of experience, are presented by the educational bodies as universally valid and universally enforceable. This is bureaucratic teaching which if geared to untalented pupils and unimaginative teachers, may destroy enthusiasm, curiosity and individual inventiveness.

b) *Tone*. In traditional teaching the ear was judged by its ability to recognize rhythm on the one hand and pitch (melody) on the other. In fact, a significant aspect of aural ability is sensitivity to tone colour. Its presence or absence has a great influence and plays a decisive role both in truly rhythmic playing and in melodic phrasing and harmonic execution. The beauty of tone-colour depends not only on the quality of the instrument, but also—despite the theories worked out by physicists a few decades ago denying the possibility of its effect on tone-colour—on the imagination of the performer. (More will be said on this in Chapter IV.) Depending on his ability to produce varying tone-colours, the performer can produce marvellous effects of touch that extend the colour-scale of the performance almost limitlessly. Who can say how this comes about, when it has been physically demonstrated that touch on the piano can only be affected in terms of dynamics? The arguments of Tetzel and other physicists do not concern the teacher. He or she is primarily a musician, who has to acquire musical conceptions on the highest possible level, realize them on his instrument—and teach them to others. He will find out how to achieve this by turning for advice not to physicists or mathematicians but to good performers and above all, to good pieces. He must examine well-constructed music, and be able to hear it with his inner ear, and then—provided he has an adequate technique—it will sound as he imagined it. If the teacher has a good relationship with his pupil, and the pupil has the same with the music, then the pupil, too, will come to play it correctly. How does this happen? Using which muscles? Who cares?! A music teacher is not a physicist, not an anatomist, not even a sports coach. According to Martienssen, it is "irrational", that despite all physical evidence a piano sounds totally different when an artist plays from when a strummer strums. Perhaps it is irrational, perhaps we have simply not yet found the key to it—it does not matter. We must play good music, conceive it well, and be able to play the piano—and if the instrument is a good one which conforms to the dictates of an expert musical imagination, physical processes will be of little interest. This is not a question of science but of artistic imagination. It cannot be transferred from one artist's playing to another's, nor can a pupil copy it. Everyone must struggle on his own for imagination and its proper implementation. What the teacher can—indeed, must—do is to arouse his pupil's sense of tone-colour from the very first lessons. These senses, linked to those for phrasing, are as equally susceptible to development as any other aspect of ear-training. Apart from rhythm, tone-colour is the most important sense of all. It is extremely important to realize, however, that a sense of tone is not to be kindled through touch; beauty of touch must develop from musical imagination and musical phrasing. Desire for musical beauty must dictate beauty of touch, for tonal sense is only of any use if it is not directed at individual notes but promotes beautiful music-making.

3 Music—its content and form

The music teacher must not only feel music, he must perceive its essence as well. Music is the only audibly perceived art, just as the fine arts are understood on a purely visual basis. Today the fine arts can no longer be regarded as purely "descriptive", although not long ago people who looked at pictures were interested primarily in what the picture "portrayed". And although even today the great majority of laymen do not know what to make of a picture whose immediate subject cannot be recognized, those who teach art can be presumed and expected not to teach the art of seeing solely or even primarily in figurative form. Everyone except the blind can look, but very few see, and the art of seeing must (or should) be included in aesthetic education in schools.

The same applies to the field of ear-training in music. Only the layman thinks music is the most abstract of arts. It is characteristic not only of music but of every art that when viewed or listened to superficially, they do not offer up their charms on a silver platter. (This is why *Gesamtkunst*—total art—is impracticable, for few people can completely absorb even one art-form.)

At the time when dilettantism blossomed, coming into fashion with "mass musical education" as its byword, there were a lot of arguments about the content of music. Many music educators at that time mistakenly interpreted the expression "content" as being the music's "programme"—its story or even just its emotions. Of course, all art stems from the creator's emotions, or is at least filled with them. The performer assumes these emotions, or shapes them to his own image, and the listener does the same in his own way. This is how the activities of the creative and re-creative artists and the art-lovers form a whole. The emotions are, however, only giving outward expression to the music's content. Even in Romantic works, joy and sorrow are not the content, simply its manifestation, in the same way as the "story" is not the content of poetry. It is still more obvious that music's content is not the action it may underlie—not even in opera—but the masterly shaping of musical material. Even in popular music love is not the content, only the text. In both cases the music always shapes itself, and the fact that it may thereby provide a background to some action or feeling from another form of art—or trash—is not its essence. The music of a song is formed in itself without the words. The "musical content" of Schubert's "The Trout" does not differ from that of the "Trout Quintet" because the song is a background to the trout's swift swimming—an essential illustration in the song—while in the quintet this illustration is not brought to the fore. It differs because in "The Trout" Schubert created a work according to the laws of song, whereas in the quintet he wrote for five instruments, where a piano and string quartet, and not a voice with accompanying piano, interplay according to the laws of the given music.

So what are the laws of music's construction that determine the content?

Music can only be explained with music. For music to be produced, rhythm, melody, beat, form, etc. must be felt. A random succession of notes is not a melody, nor does the random accumulation of notes of varying length and loudness provide rhythm. Notes only produce music when they follow each other logically within a certain system—which can be called style—and thereby mass together into some sort of form or formal elements.

Rhythm: a coherent, and thus systematically organized group of notes of varying length and intensity. Melody: a coherent, and thus systematically organized group of notes of varying pitch.

A good melody or rhythm is one whose notes are linked together with convincing logic in accordance with one style.

As the piece unfolds the individual notes and motives merge and inter-react on each other to form larger units which in turn are interdependent and gradually give the piece its final form.

It is this indissoluble interdependence that determines how music should be taught. Only when we see the various parts of a piece of music in their interdependence, and make others see this, are we really teaching music. Making it into a whole can only be done if we feel the dividing lines between the individual parts. Only something which is intelligently divided up can be intelligently brought together. Making the division, however, does not mean complete dismemberment—it is they that do the linking. A period, for instance, can only be brought together if this also involves construction. We should feel, and make others feel, that the second part is answering the first. Performing music means following and interpreting its evolving form. This may be an instinctive emotional reaction on the part of the performer—this may be true of the very talented pupil, too—but the teacher must be aware of the music's evolving form, or he will not be able to teach it to those who cannot find it for themselves.

One note on its own is not enough to be called music, but even several notes will only constitute music if they group together according to certain laws, and stand in some relationship to each other. Therefore the way music is shaped not only determines its content, but also provides its substance.

Man's taste at different periods of time has grouped notes according to some sort of law, depending on its state of development, in a number of different ways; in respect of pitch this occurs both vertically and horizontally. The notes are drawn towards or repel each other, divide up and then join, taking shape melodically and harmonically. This is the prerequisite if certain sounds are to be called music. The dialectic of the formation of music is as follows: a work of music consists of sections that are distinguished from each other (centrifugal force) but that refer to each other (centripetal force).

In a good work, these two forces keep each other balanced, and a good performance will show this. Only divisions that are clearly distinguished can be linked together; I can only make connections where I perceive the structural lay-out. In music formed in this way, every note has its function, and this is why the music is intelligible. Of course, if intelligibly fashioned music is to sound intelligible, the performer, too, must know—or at least feel—what the music's content is, i.e. the way the material has been shaped.

The shaping of the material derives from a system of answer, with one motive answering another, and groups of motives answering each other over an ever widening area; the parts, the movements all consist of answers. A good performance, in which every facet of the music helps the other and rhythm, dynamics, agogics, melody and chordal harmony together express the unravelling of the form, brings this system out. This is the music's essence, and it can be understood and read from the score.

This is what can and must be taught. The meaningfulness of the rhythm, melody, harmony, attraction and repulsion, etc., contained in the score, and whose smallest intricacies the teacher must track down to the limits of possibility. This is the job of recreative art and it can be enhanced by teaching. The teacher's job is to indicate to his pupil why a musical work or idea is beautiful. To achieve this, he must be a good and understanding musician. (For example, a musical idea is beautiful *in the first place* because its construction, the melodic line, the sequence of harmonies, the modulations, the statements and answers, etc., are logical and purposeful; and *in the second place,* as a consequence of this, it expresses certain deeply-felt or evocative emotions. The logic of the construction *must be grasped,* and at the same time the emotions can be adopted or transformed to suit one's own being—for those who have the appropriate feelings.) This can be demonstrated even to pupils who have no talent, if they have a certain sense for music which the teacher himself may well have aroused. They will then at least play intelligently, and maybe even musically, since they will understand the work in musical terms. If a pupil is talented, however, he will not only reproduce intelligently and musically what he has understood, but respond emotionally to the work the composer's emotions have brought forth. His playing will be full of life, exciting, breath-taking. This, however, cannot be taught: it is a question of talent. "*Objectivity*" *in music-making belongs to those who have not sufficient talent to recreate clearly fashioned music with feeling.*

Here we must consider one of the most exciting tasks facing performer and teacher alike, one that is raised by the polysemantism (diversity of meaning) of music. Sadly—or fortunately—music is not straightforward; and the better the music, the less so it is. This diversity is what distinguishes Bach from Gurlitt, and even from the early works of the great Viennese masters. This is why the child Mozart does not lead to the *Magic Flute,* and why a child brought up on pastiches has such enormous difficulty when confronted with Bach. The polysemantism of music must be squarely faced when the pupil begins learning, so that he will become aware of it, grow accustomed to the variety, and feel the lack of it in slipshod, flat, and unimaginative "light music"—and even in the good imitators (Türk, Kuhlau, etc.).

The role of teaching here is not easy. Children love the primitive, the straightforward, even the stupid. (Viz. "Chopsticks".) If we do not, at the earliest opportunity, get them accustomed to polysemantic music, which cannot simply be ground out but needs resolving, then sooner or later they will get tired of lightweight classical and pre-classical dances—and that will be the end of it. They will be bored with the old and neither able nor willing to understand the new. Everything else sounds strange or even out of tune to their ears.

Naturalistic teaching

Returning to our analysis of meaningful music teaching, it must also be noted that a colourful interpretation of music is not to be taught with stories or emotional exaggerations. Emotion and formal content operate mutually on one another. There is no doubt that composers derive their impulse from some sort of emotion. If they have talent, and are able to realize their musical imagination in melodic and rhythmic inventiveness, colourful harmonization and polysemantic sensibility, they will—providing their palpitating emotional world is kept in order by a controlled ability for shaping acquired through serious effort—produce a masterpiece. Thus talent and knowledge can only create a masterpiece together. This also applies to the performer, but in a different order. He interprets, re-creates the work. So first he gets to know the completed work, and comes to understand its musical content, knowing it better and better the more thoroughly he studies it. As we have seen, the musical content can be deduced and learnt from the score; but the extent to which this content inspires the performer's own feelings and the manner in which it does so, will depend on his emotional richness, his imagination, his attitude to rhythm, his sensitivity to polysemantism, in short on his talent—but this cannot be taught. I can and must draw my pupil's attention to the way the music takes shape, the way the composer's talent manifests itself, through the passed on emotions, but I cannot explain emotions or make him feel them. I can supply knowledge, if the pupil is receptive, but not talent. I cannot explain the emotional content with bursts of enthusiasm or encouragement, or with comparisons drawn from nature; and even emotional excerpts from the composer's life produce effects of equally doubtful value.

We do not need to get to know a composer from the story of his life—that's his own private affair—but from his œuvre, which he too regarded as common property. And his works actually give a better picture of him, bring him closer as a person to the pupil, than biographical writings of doubtful authenticity.

(All this does not mean that we should totally refrain from the occasional well-placed emotional or pictorial comment. There is no need to be purists. But in principle we should not rely on them but rather on the concrete facts that can be found in the score.)

III THE CHILD

All education is in fact preparation for the community. Someone living alone on an uninhabited island would not need to be educated.

1 Musical instruction and child mentality

Music teaching has two main components: the music and the pupil. These are of equal importance. In pedagogical terms, music has meaning only if it represents the human ideal, and the pupil's achievements have meaning only if as a consequence of this they are at the service of music. The teacher's work is determined by these twin components; for if he either has no feeling for music or does not understand a child's mentality, the results of his teaching will be questionable to say the least. If he has a feel for teaching and can establish a relationship with a child, but does not respond to music, then he is just as unsuitable for music teaching as if he were immensely musical but neither knew nor perhaps even cared how a child can be musically educated.

The teacher must therefore have a very sound knowledge of both *music* and *children*. Music we have dealt with in the preceding chapter.

What are the essential criteria of childhood?

The main characteristic of a healthy child is his egocentricity: he expects the world to revolve around him, and since the very manifestation of life is a great experience for him, he constantly wants to give *signs of life;* he derives great joy from using his barely developed organs as much as possible. So he is always making a noise and moving about. It is education's job to bring all these activities to order. We cannot make a present to the child of basic characteristics or force them upon him. We can only—either well or badly—direct those that are already there. Well, if we know the talent characteristics and can find the ways and means of putting them in order and developing them; badly, if we do not develop them, or if we suppress them, wishing to force our own conceptions on him instead. We can do no more than develop his abilities and set them off in the right direction, counterbalancing those characteristics—notably so-called inhibitions—which have a harmful effect on life's course and are the greatest obstacles to a child's development. In nearly every case the cause of the child's inhibitions is aggressive interference alien to his na-

24

ture and inclinations; it can range widely from gentle but persistent persuasion to brutality, but is very dangerous in all its manifestations. The ways in which inhibitions are expressed vary enormously, from dare-nothing self-depreciation to the most aggressive big-headedness.

Thus the popular comparison with tree-pruning is both misleading and dangerous. A tree has no self-awareness and no nervous system; if we cut some part of it away, we do not create inhibitions and make it unsure of itself.

Aggressive interference can cause damage that will last a lifetime. If we try and suppress some "flaw" in the child in this way, it will appear elsewhere, perhaps in a more dangerous form; if we force him to behave in a way we consider correct but which goes against his nature, he will become rebellious, defiant or untruthful.

Teaching is guiding

This is why a teacher's responsibilities are so enormous. As if all pupils could be treated in the same way, with commands and measures worked out in advance! In that case, everything could be learnt at teachers' training college, and it would just depend on the prospective teacher's diligence in swotting up the instructions. (Sadly, in many places this is what people think; they ignore the fact that children are living creatures with independent minds and nervous systems.)

A child demands to be taken notice of, but does not accept this from everyone. To this end his love, trust and respect must be won, and they can only be won if we show interest in him but refrain overdoing our approach with endearments or condescension. As far as possible one should wait for the child to make the approaches, which usually happens quite soon if we do not force matters, for the child is curious to know what we want of him. Once this has happened, the relationship must be maintained in a serious but cheerful atmosphere. And we will only acquire authority by not climbing on to a pedestal, and refusing to argue, but by admitting the errors we may make and discussing the reasons for them with the child. Thereafter—once we have got to know each other a little—the next most important thing is to be consistent, for educating children is based not on persuasion but on conditioning. This is the value of setting an example—instructions should not be rigid and relentless, but consistent. Children do not like instructions and are not very fond of advice. They react instinctively against orders (though there are some children of "bureaucratic" disposition who supplement their lack of imagination by imitating) while in reality they require order and organization, for otherwise they do not feel solid ground beneath their feet. They will do anything to be in the right, but will feel more secure if the person in charge of them demonstrates that he is right. (Not, of course, with explanations, but by practical illustration.) This is why they generally like strict but fair teachers. What they abhor most is compulsory exertion; not the exertion itself, for their whole existence consists of practice—they practise speaking, walking, jumping, throwing, spinning round, doing handstands, spitting—they spend all day practising. But not compulsorily: they see the sense and the object of what they are doing, and so *make an effort voluntarily*.

How can such activity be harnessed for the purposes of teaching?

This is education's biggest problem: the answer is different for every child. One way is certainly wrong: deliberate attempts at persuasion, appealing to the child's mind. This will not interest him in the least. Children are not even prepared to learn lessons from fairy-tales, though they are fond of them and their sense of fairness responds to the lessons they contain, and they would lose their taste for them if the moral did not satisfy their sense of fairness; but this fairness has nothing to do with their own lives: the rewarding of virtue, the punishment of wickedness, the results of hard work and the losses due to laziness can be equally credible or incredible to them as the seven-headed dragon, and have no effect on the rhythm of their lives. The dispensation of justice is fairy-tale, too. On the other hand, the effect on children of the bear brushing her teeth every day in TV story time* is very typical and worth considering. It is not the instructive larks and remarks of Rascal and Raisin that get the lesson across, but the pleasantly dramatized brushing of the teeth repeated at exactly the same time day after day.

The dispensation of justice a child comes across in his own life has no moral content for him either. He knows why reward and punishment occur, because he has got used to it. But he does not really understand what in the eyes of adults is good or bad in his behaviour, he just gets used to the fact that a certain action or conduct, for example, always results in punishment, and gradually he comes to believe that it is bad; explanations are quite superfluous, he still will not understand why it is bad. He cannot be expected to perceive, for instance, how much effort and money it costs his parents to decorate the home and keep it nice; he finds a room turned inside out much more interesting than a neat row of toys, and a cushion cut up with scissors much more fun than a clean, whole one. He can only *get used* to order, if he has it consistently applied. The capacity for *persuasion* has not developed in a child, so it is impossible to *persuade* him with reasons. A child's ethics are not based on conviction but on tradition—he doesn't think about it, he believes it, because he's used

---

*A daily programme on Hungarian Television is the "Bedtime Story", which is switched on by a bear. But first she does a few exercises, brushes her teeth and puts on a nightgown to a bassoon accompaniment.

to the fact that this is how it is at home or at school. If the consistency comes to a halt, however—two sides try to influence him in differing directions, either at home or at school—then the continuous habit-forming process will be interrupted, it will lose its effect, and the child's moral foundations will be shattered. Clearly, under such conditions the child cannot be expected to "respect" those influencing him, particularly if he realizes they are in opposition to each other. In contrast to this, consistency is supremely impressive, as he feels that he will come under its influence to such a degree that there will be no escape. And while he is afraid of powerful influences that fence him in, he also needs them, for he is aware of his own weakness and lack of direction. This he finds very disturbing. And if he does not receive strong guidance from some quarter or other, he will escape into exaggerated cockiness and insolent conceitedness.

Children can also suffer from the feeling of inferiority, which is really lack of confidence. This is extremely harmful in all its manifestations, and leaves its mark on all the child's activities, also determining, among other things, his attitude towards learning. Searching out its origins, diagnosing it, is not easy for the music teacher, as his relationship with his pupil is fairly loose—he sees him twice a week on average—and countless circumstances can hinder or completely nullify any influence he might have. We might think of the over-active parents who "always know best" even where music is concerned, and impart bad influences—the direct result of a lack of self-respect—on school work, too. Even so, the music teacher can do a lot in this area. If, of necessity, he keeps parental influence separated from his own work, and can enter into a partnership with the child based on trust and mutual respect, a healthy confidence will develop within the child which may result in the lessening or perhaps the disappearance of his self-depreciation.

Confidence cannot be likened to conceit—it is precisely the opposite. Conceit is the over-compensation of *self-depreciation,* while confidence is the outward sign of *psychological equilibrium.* As we shall see later, just as in physical terms, physical balance is the most important factor in learning an instrument, so in terms of every kind of intellectual and ethical development, etc., psychological equilibrium is what is most important. The pupil must know his own value, and this is what the teacher must call on. Liszt's immortal observation: "noblesse oblige", is the most appropriate attitude towards learning. Talent obliges! The more talented the pupil is, the more we can demand of him by referring to this and calling on his own awareness. But only if he is aware of his talent and adapts all his activity to this loftier ability. To a lesser extent this awakening of equilibrium can apply to every child, which does not of course mean that the less talented a pupil is, the lower the level of demands we make upon him in human terms. Self-esteem can be made into the basic factor in learning in every child, for under normal conditions it is an organic part of the life-instinct (think of the self-esteem in the toddling of a 2–3-year-old child when it knows for certain how to walk!). The teacher should have confidence in his pupil and respect and exploit every little success, patiently correcting mistakes and *not scolding him!*—for this will have no useful effect whatever, and will either spoil the child's love for learning or accustom him to not attending to the teacher. Mistakes should be pointed out briefly, meaningfully, and very occasionally severely.

The source of mistakes is not always insufficient practice. It often happens that the child turns up for the lesson without having practised, yet the time will be profitably spent. At other times nothing in the lesson goes right, yet the pupil has practised diligently. From this he deduces that it is not worth practising. There can be very many reasons for lessons going well or badly. When the weather is bad, not only is the teacher more impatient and nervy, but the child is also less attentive. Of course we cannot organize ourselves round this and make our results depend on the weather. At times like these the teacher must exercise self-discipline and exploit his love of teaching. If it is apparent that the child is very inattentive, one should not struggle on with the badly played set pieces but turn to something else—sight-reading, learning a new piece, or duets, talking about a concert or some other musical experience, or a bit of musical history. Happily, music is such a rich, wide field that any amount of things can be dealt with usefully. Apart from "the weather", other factors can also cause intense inattention, for instance, good or bad prospects or experiences at home or at school, or in the case of a willing child, if he sits down at the piano with a guilty conscience as a result of not having practised. This sort of bad feeling, wherever it comes from, must unfailingly be removed—its causes discussed with the child (without scolding or reproach)—if possible in such a way that the result is not dejection but a determination that the next lesson will certainly be better. Sometimes, of course, we have to speak our minds strongly, but this should always be *brief* and to the point, focussing on what is essential, without anger, and preferably with humour. (This last is especially useful with adolescent boys.) And we should never, never say to the child: "You ought to be ashamed of yourself!" To begin with, he is not ashamed. And if he were, it would be a very bad thing. He should not practise out of shame, or vanity, for good marks, or to please his teacher. We must succeed in getting him under music's spell, and his curiosity about music will lead him to practise. If we do not achieve this at some stage or other, then all our efforts will have been in vain. It can even be achieved with the non-musical child, provided it is what guides us, and provided our interest and love of both music and the child are in equilibrium.

If we do not take all this into account, it is quite conceivable that lasting opposition (aggression) will develop in the child. Aggression is the child's revenge on the person bringing him up. He may bring the foundation for it from home or school, but music teaching can exacerbate or mitigate this unpleasant behaviour to a considerable degree. Sadly, the former is the more common case, though one of music teaching's most important tasks ought to be the latter. The reasons why aggression and inhibitions develop are identical. In both cases they are the result of a lack of equilibrium in the psychic, physical, or some other sphere. A child who feels he is deprived of affection is mistrustful; he approaches everything new without confidence. A child whose capabilities are not sufficiently recognized makes an abnormal attempt to call attention to himself, behaves noisily and aggressively, and wants to produce an effect at all costs; if he can't be the best, the cleverest, the most adept, he will play the part of the worst, clumsiest and most stupid "dunce" in revenge.

To a certain extent everyone is "playing a part".

Generally speaking, adults mould their parts to their own convictions, and either perfect and deepen them, or make them automatic through practice. The former is wise, humane, and concerned with essentials, the latter superficial and perhaps deliberately aiming to deceive. But at all events a part is created, whether it is that of Diogenes or of a charlatan; a great actor or a ham. Of course, the two can get mixed up. Small children already have role-playing tendencies, and the teacher can exploit this too, mainly by example. He must choose the right ideal to suit the role played by the child.

The role-playing tendency is at its strongest during adolescence, which finds its most striking manifestation in fashion-worship. With time it grows more discreet, more profound, in many respect under the influence of education. (Of course there are those who are still "adolescents" at the age of sixty.)

The music teacher can be of enormous help here, for he is a principal agent and representative of emotional upbringing. In many cases, whether the child's development into an adult takes an honest or dishonest form will depend on the influence of the music teacher.

2 Teaching beginners

Teaching beginners is the most exciting stage of music teaching. It is exciting first and foremost because it involves enormous responsibility; success in all kinds of work depends primarily on the grounding. Where the basis is insecure or deformed, there can be no question of further progress under normal conditions; on the other hand, one can always return to a sound basis, even after possible excursions on the wrong path.

It is exciting in the second place because if the grounding is properly accomplished, it excludes routine work.

During the first weeks and months every single pupil has to be treated differently, and at the same time one has to discover what features they may have in common. During this period we still know nothing concrete about the child, at most we may suspect something on the basis of our former experiences that enables us to work out what must be done. This period demands such constant and unwavering attention from the teacher that there can be no question of boredom or fatigue. The unwavering attention should not appear in activity but in discovering possible ways of leading the child towards music. The teacher crouches and waits like a spider in a web; he does not fight or struggle or give orders or argue, he rather pounces on the slightest movement and exploits it at once with care and understanding. The aim of getting nearer the child may—indeed should—be determined. The objectives set out may be precise, but the means thereto, the way they are used and the time they take cannot be determined in advance. These change minute by minute according to whether the web is quivering or motionless. Teaching beginners is exciting and varied because no two children are alike, and every instant differs from the next. The excitement is like that of the hunter, and equally intense, but vastly superior in its results, for it is directed not towards killing, but towards life's most wonderful aspect: the creation of a human being's relationship with art.

In Martienssen's view, the starting-point for teaching should be the way a child prodigy approaches music. And however surprising this statement may appear at first sight, it is almost 100 per cent accurate, and not completely 100 per cent, for the reason that there are no perfectly watertight truths in teaching; and one of the greatest dangers, if not the greatest, is when we believe that something is universally applicable, and act accordingly.

But how far is Martienssen correct in the comment noted above? Up to the age of about 10 (it is impossible to fix a precise time-limit, of course) the normal child has no propensity towards abstraction, for he is incapable of grasping abstract concepts. Just as primitive man needs to personalize abstract concepts in order to find some way of approaching them so the child, too, can only grasp concrete things. Everything he cannot follow with his sense he does under duress, which is why he either alters it according to his liking, avoids it, or rejects it decisively and often rudely. If he has been frightened, he may learn it off pat without any understanding. This is the most dangerous thing of all, as it will determine his way of learning in the future, and systematically accustom him to not thinking.

But there are certain abstractions at the beginning of music teaching that cannot, according to the traditional view, be avoided. These include score-reading, for instance, or the visual registration of music, on the one hand; and the conscious memorizing of certain positions, on the other: the relationship of the hand, arm, and shoulder to the keyboard, the determining of the sitting position, distance and balance, or certain movements, such as the guiding of the upper arm along the keyboard, the fall of the arm, the raising of the fingers, and the striking of the keys. The correct solution to all these tasks is dependent on intellectual requirements; and while they are physical, they can only be brought about by attention, i.e. with the aid of intellectual activity.

Martienssen's conception of the above is based on his conclusions from the fairly comprehensive material left concerning Mozart as a child, as a result of which he emphasizes that the viewpoint in music teaching which claims that the child prodigy is a very rare phenomenon and can therefore be ignored is totally false. In his view, the methods used to teach every child should be based on the behaviour of the prodigy, for it is he, albeit unconsciously, who unerringly *feels* how to tackle music. And the pattern for initiating every child into the secrets of music should be what the child prodigy does *instinctively*. The young Mozart went to the piano, violin and organ *voluntarily*, and discovered the joys of playing without being shown. His father took care not to interfere until a good while later, when gradually and continuously, alongside his son's own music-making, he set about approaching the abstract elements. In the same way we should wait for the appropriate time with every child—and of course this will generally take much longer than with the child prodigy. During this period the teacher should note and exploit the "quiverings" on the web. When the young Mozart first sat down at the piano, his hand position, balance and distance of his body from the instrument were certainly not perfect. No one expected that of him. When the time came, his father clearly dealt with it. But by that time the ear element was predominant in his piano-playing.

And what about the normal child?

How can the child prodigy syndrome be adapted to the average child's pattern of development?

The first thing to do is to establish the steps a child prodigy takes instinctively, without outside interference, when starting to play the piano.

He goes to the piano out of spontaneous curiosity, to coax sounds out of it—it does not matter if they are single notes or a tune he has heard or imagined. To begin with he will generally pay more attention to single notes or clusters of notes, as he finds the sound itself more interesting than a completed tune, which he would be more likely to sing. So in producing the notes he already has certain demands in terms of sound. How the notes are produced, as a problem, never occurs to him, in the same way as a child does not reflect on his muscular functions before reaching out for some object. He simply stretches out his hand and takes it. (Who would dream of making sure that this happens with the correct and most suitable movements? In practice the child will discover for itself how to take hold of an object.) Thus, the urge to produce a note is what sets the movement going. This movement may be correct or incorrect in functional terms, but of course that will be of no concern to the child, whose attention is devoted to the sound. Producing the sound is deliberate; the way it is done is, however, an instinctive, subconscious operation. The next stage is adjusting the sound; this can influence the functioning of the movement, and after a certain amount of practice will influence it, again instinctively and without outside prompting. Instinctively, of its own accord and not of course, according to the norms preconceived by the teacher, the movement will get nearer and nearer the rational and effective process of piano-playing. And as spontaneous and voluntary movements are not stiff, the teacher can, as the need arises, mould them in due time ever closer to an appropriate treatment of the piano. But what if the child does not possess this inborn musicality, if he has no spontaneous desire to produce sounds on the piano? Can this be replaced by abstractions, or by something which the above observations indicate are off-putting?

There are various ways of arousing enthusiasm in the piano (the most suitable being preparatory training*); thereafter we can gather experiences concerning the child's budding musicality by observing the quiverings on the web, and on the basis of these store up our experiences in this direction, so that we can make use of them at the appropriate moment. How many apparently fruitless lessons can go by before a useful intervention occurs successfully in this direction and all of a sudden something opens up and finds an echo in numerous previous, cautious attempts! The teacher must be infinitely patient in waiting for this, bearing in mind that "grass grows as a result of suitable conditions and care, and not from being pulled!"

(The way a non-musical child of developed intelligence starts learning can suffice as an example that the Martienssen adaptation of the child prodigy situation is not the best solution in every case at the outset of teaching; in many cases the non-musical child is incapable of imagining music or indeed of repeating a given note. Children like this with a "dud ear" can have greater success in approaching music through their intelligence, insofar as they are capable of certain abstractions, than through being forced into singing and spotaneous imagining. Children like this do not even want to sing, since they can hear they are out of tune and are ashamed of it, and would rather stop

---

*In Hungary, in all the state and cooperative private music schools, the children spend a year on a preliminary course before starting to learn an instrument; there, singing and playing in groups, they get a grasp of the basics: solmisation, rhythm, beat, etc.

learning music. In such cases we can bring the visual–intellectual side to the foreground and rest assured that the child will comprehend music at a later date through this; in this way he can reach music more easily and effectively. But this method should only be used as a last resort, when it is perfectly plain that we will not get anywhere with primary musical effects.)

From the first lessons we must work out what can be expected of the child, and what the minimum is that we can build upon in terms of a) mechanics, b) ear, and c) knowledge.

In times past, piano teaching took no account of the child's temperament; and in the belief that it was easier to play slowly than to play fast, tried to make the beginning easier by adopting the slowest possible speeds. In doing so it underestimated or rather misunderstood children's powers of comprehension, did not take their needs into account, wasted their previous musical experiences, if any, and aimed at some sort of completely new visual-motorial conditioning that hardly came near music at all. Nowadays piano teaching all over the world has discarded these old practices whereby the child began his learning with finger exercises followed by unison passages in semi-breves.

The child needs elementary training before beginning on an instrument, the task of which is to provide him with musical experiences on which instrumental study can later build. Play songs and children's songs used in elementary training and which today are used at the beginning of piano teaching are to be played at singing speed and thus correspond to the child's powers of comprehension. In this way teaching does not put a brake on what is most important—the child's impetus and his musical needs—but exploits them. This impetus is virtually irretrievable in further musical studies if its course is once interrupted by incorrect teaching.

a) *How can natural technique be developed?*

Before a child begins playing the piano, he has already used his arms, hands and fingers for many different movements. These, however, were fundamentally at variance with the movements required for piano-playing. Up till now, the child has generally used his hands with the palms facing each other. The rotation of the forearm by which we bring the arm and hand into the right position for the keyboard, is a movement very rarely used by children and not a natural one. This is the first difficulty in piano-playing and to begin with the most troublesome. But there are many others. For instance, up till now the child has not been hindered in any of his activities if his finger-joints caved in or his wrist and elbow did not "support" his hand, etc. For the child, these demands are new and not "natural". The teacher must not be impatient but must find a way of slowly and gradually arriving at the desired adjustment.

Forcibly demanding this new and rapid conditioning is also one of the brakes that can bring the child's initial impetus to a halt. But there are also new ways of moving which are "natural", and we can be more strict in our demands here. Among these are the correct functioning of the arm as it falls, feeling with the tips of the fingers when two or three fingers are in play, a slight raising of the fingers, and the "transfer" from one finger to the next; we can also expect that when they play with five fingers together (a pentachord), their fingers will feel the five keys and their hand will not slide about, close up or stretch too far out. These are demands which are no different from the natural movements they have already used. If possible, however, as we introduce the new movements carefully and link them to demands in terms of sound, we should not repress the existing, natural movements, on the contrary, we should exploit them to the full, since they are relaxed and thus extremely valuable.

We can state quite boldly that the average child is much more dexterous and resourceful in his movements than is actually required in the teaching of beginners even today. It is just that he is dexterous in a different way, as his movements have been conditioned from another aspect. It is the duty of the teacher, and one which requires enormous patience, to find out just how much and how fast this dexterity can be made use of with each child. If we want to induce the child to play the piano according to certain technical norms, his individual dexterity and resourcefulness will never become apparent and will be wasted.

b) *How can the ear be developed?*

What can we expect of the child in musical terms when we start teaching him the piano? It cannot be stressed frequently and emphatically enough just how important preliminary classes are from this point of view. Even if these classes only get through the minimum of material and if the children have not really "learnt" anything there. They will undoubtedly have got to know a number of children's songs, will certainly have walked and moved to rhythm, and will, even in the poorest of classes, have got an inkling of solmisation. This is crucial! In the preliminary course the child will acquire *some* kind of musical experience and will have *some* idea that music has a certain order, regularity, and high and low, long and short notes. And he will have got used to this in a group, working with others. This is enough for us to recognize preliminary classes as indispensable. The emphasis is on the fact that all this takes place in a group, not consciously, not compulsorily, but as a game, and thus spontaneity is assured under all circumstances. With individual instrumental lessons this effect is virtually unattainable.

c) What can we expect in terms of knowledge?

Very little. As has been pointed out more fully above, a 7–8-year-old child is not a rational being, and acquires information in life through his instincts and sense organs rather than through thinking. In the following 1–2 years we should not expect much development in this field either. The less we explain and the more we encourage music-making, the better. From the outset we should strive for musically accurate performances and meaningful phrasing, but we should endeavour to achieve this not with explanations but by encouraging a feeling for the music. It will be no use, for instance, if the child can work out the beat correctly in its head, but cannot play it in time.

The idea that the movements and postures the child uses spontaneously can have a bad effect on future technical development is quite erroneous. It is the movements and postures that have been wrongly adopted as a result of the teacher's instructions that have a bad effect. Stiffness and unnatural attitudes will only come about if they are forced on the child. What the child does "in error" in his own experiments as he gets to know the piano will leave no trace in his future playing since it is not forced, indoctrinated or stiff; and as his demands in terms of sound develop he will soon realize that what he invents in order to be able to pick out a tune is not the way to play the piano.

Let's take a concrete common example: a slightly-built child of seven or eight sits down at the piano to tap out a tune he's heard. Let's try to imagine how this child views the world. Because his fingers are so weak, he has to struggle with the keys to make them work—only his desire for sound drives him to find a solution. Up till this point in his life he has only been able to use force by swinging the upper half of his body to *strike* something; by kicking with the lower half of his body; or by using all his strength to *grasp hold* of something. Naturally enough, he did this in a relaxed and supple posture, since the movement was instinctive and unforced. A child will only produce stiffness—i.e. the unproductive and senseless conflict between two opposing groups of muscles—if it is forced on him from outside. (Who ever saw a child wave with a stiff arm?) *Instinctive movements are relaxed.* The child crouches at the piano and strikes the keys with his hands and arms held completely wrong, *thinking only of the sound!* And if, with time, we endeavour to change his posture (through some enjoyable exercises, perhaps), the concentration on the musical sound and the relaxed movement must be maintained at all costs, and nothing should distract his attention from it. This is the same for the child prodigy. If we refrain from forcing him into a posture that conforms to our own preconceptions, we shall avoid the greatest danger, stiffness. The remaining "mistakes", like the drooping of the hand, the caving-in of the fingers, etc., will disappear sooner or later (in a couple of months or perhaps 1–2 years) as the child grows larger and stronger, provided his *demands in terms of sound have been in the forefront of his learning,* and provided corrections have been made carefully, logically and gently, in a flexible and not preconceived manner.

When music teaching begins, however—at least when traditional piano teaching begins—there are certain abstract ideas which cannot be dispensed with for long: for example, the inculcation of a sense of pitch and rhythm. How does the music teacher using traditional methods behave here? He uses complicated stories, diversions which interest the child and achieve apparent success, but do not bring the music at all nearer the child.

There are birds and birds' nests drawn on the stave, verses used to help memorize the theoretical knowledge, and pictures and stories full of atmosphere, etc. These have the sole and very dubious merit of amusing the child. They may possibly strengthen the teacher's relationship with him, but there are better, truer and more musical means to that end; I shall come to them later.

As I have mentioned, in the course of learning generally, but especially during the first lessons, it is the pupil, and not the teacher, who needs to be the more active. Good conductors also talk little, move economically, and let the orchestra do the work, or rather, induce it to work. It is striking that the really great conductors—like Ansermet, Klemperer or Frigyes Reiner—were able to whip the orchestra up to the highest pitch with an absolute minimum of movement. For this, of course, authority is needed as well as knowledge. The same is true of the music teacher. If he talks, explains, sings, prescribes and declaims, he will bore and upset the child, who, if he is longing for music, will want to work everything out and put it into practice for himself. This sounds high-flown, of course, and would not occur in the beginner's mind; it is only in the ensuing results that the damage done by keeping the child in the background, and the extreme usefulness of letting him experiment freely, will become apparent. The child must be left free—but not, of course, left completely alone. We should never prescribe things, but rather wait and see what the child discovers itself, and only interfere cautiously if what he is doing goes against the presumable run of development. What it is that goes against this cannot be unambiguously determined, and it will be referred to in a later chapter.

Neuhaus has written: "Believe me, playing the piano is easy..."—and he wasn't only thinking of the most gifted people. And it is a fact: playing the piano is easy—at the appropriate level and according to one's ability—provided we do not make it difficult. And everyone enjoys playing the piano—provided we do not take their pleasure away.

This is the basic problem in teaching beginners.

IV PSYCHOLOGICAL REQUIREMENTS

1 The revision of piano teaching methods

"It is not the fault of canned music and the radio if learning to play the piano is losing popularity today; it is primarily and almost exclusively the result of uncreative piano teaching" writes Martienssen in his basic work on piano teaching.

After criticizing traditional methods of piano teaching, he goes on to indicate the correct path: "For a long time it was a principle of piano teaching that the basis of its organization could only be physiological. Every detailed work on piano teaching began with a thorough grounding in physiology. A certain knowledge of anatomy was indispensable for the piano teacher. Technique was considered an ability independent of art and the artist's personality and something that could be passed on mechanically, using purely external means." What is needed is for "piano teaching to make a sharp turn in its attitudes from the chiefly physiological to the chiefly psychological. In place of technical instruction from the outside inwards, a sort of teaching should come into effect which works from the inside outwards."

If the piano is to regain its standing and piano teaching its reputation, it is absolutely essential for piano-teaching methods to be modernized in this spirit.

The chiefly physiological outlook outlined by Martienssen has happily shifted somewhat nearer to music in recent times, both in piano-teaching theory—which is sadly very incomplete and fortuitously and subjectively conceived—and in practice. And this has happened as a result of the upsurge in mass teaching amid fierce opposition from the old school, who feared that technical grounding would diminish with the greater intrusion of music.

For all its usefulness, however, this welcome musical influence has not been able to bring about a revision of methods, precisely because it was devoid of any kind of logical expression, or solid foundations that have matured through the exchange of ideas. What it achieved, it accomplished as the fruit of the mass-movement that got under way on the basis of an instinctive musical longing, Kodály's principle of "music belongs to everybody", and not in order to satisfy the peremptory demands of instrumental teaching. Consequently, what piano teaching achieved through the influence of mass demand, it will soon lose, if things are allowed to continue, due to too great emphasis on thorough technical training. In teaching, too, revolutionary elements help each other by progressing side by side, and an extremely fruitful development can evolve from their effect on each other, as happened in the case of our revolution in general music teaching. If, however, after thorough argument and evaluation, the theoretical basis is not consciously laid down, the achievements will prove insecure; and if the bad traditions of the past are not defeated for all time with both arguments and results, they still have considerable strength at their disposal to return, stamp out the achievements and obliterate what was good.

The old, outdated methods should be attacked from the psychological rather than the musical side, and its outdated arguments refuted with psychological reasoning. Musical arguments are not belligerent and tangible enough to go into action against such deeply-rooted conventions, which have dominated for many decades: however much we may strive to make art easier to grasp for teaching purposes, it has no belligerent weapons at its disposal.

It isn't enough to confront physiology with musical arguments; we must resort to the forceful and unassailable weapons of psychology.

These days all over the world the psychological tendency in teaching has come to the fore—perhaps too much so. When we examine the development of a child's musical personality, we should be careful of going too far in our desire to correct the old mistakes. In the last analysis the teacher still has to keep a firm hand on the reins, even when he does not want to mould the child but simply guide him according to his aptitude. The incorrect judgement implied in the justifiably widely-held view that "one learns from other people's mistakes", is also responsible for rigidity in teaching. Since learning is at least as much an emotional as an intellectual activity, this is an inference which in education can only be used in matters of detail, and not in general. If we really want to make something our own, we have to experience it; we cannot economize on blunders and misconceptions by taking over the way others have put their failures right. In the teaching of the arts, which constitute primarily an emotional category, this is to a great extent true, and is why teaching in its restricted sense—the explanation of, and insistence on, techniques tried out and tested by others—has such little value. It is a great triumph for education and for guidance if they succeed in getting the pupil to learn from his own mistakes. This is not easy either. How much easier life would be, if we did not constantly fall back into the same old mistakes.

2 Types of ability

General pedagogy divides types of ability into three groups: visual, auditive and motoric. Music teaching adopted this dinstinction by evaluating the characteristics from musical points of view. Thus the auditive type naturally is closest to musical ability, in combination with the motoric type in the case of instrumental playing. To accept visuality as one of the constituents of musical talent is, I think, misleading. Visual experience gives a naturalistic basis to an interpretation, since providing a piece with a programme is only an attempt to supplement the musical conception through non-musical means. This is highly erroneous and harmful. If pictorial effects have a decisive influence on the emotions, they will push the musical understanding, the conscious or sub-conscious grasp of the music, into the background. Music, though, must make its impact and come across by its own means through our ears. Providing a visual programme in music teaching may enliven a momentary performance, but it will have no effect in pure musical terms. The visual can only be of help in score-reading and memorizing.

This question, of course, must not be regarded in isolation, nor must we oversimplify it; as usual with any kind of classification we need to be very careful. In every individual the different types of ability are mixed to a greater or lesser extent. It is the task of teaching to classify abilities according to their aims and exploit them appropriately.

It is my view, however, that a fourth type, the intellectual, should be included with the other three. This individual characteristic, the possessors of which are primarily thinkers and approach music through logic, cannot be ignored. And although it is commonly thought that the ideal instrumental player is the auditive type with motoric skills in support, we cannot expect much in music teaching today from pupils who lack the criteria of the intellectual type.

An awareness of type classification is pertinent to the music teacher because all type characteristics can be developed. He must take note of which type characteristics are lacking in certain pupils and which need to be developed. This, of course, can be achieved where the teaching is intuitive and personal, and not predetermined and schematic.

3 The analysis of talent

This, perhaps, is the best moment to bring up the question of talent, which is fairly unclear to a number of teachers. Yet it is exceptionally important from the point of view of assessing pupils, evaluating their present and planning their future.

Talent itself—*all* talent—is a psychological and not a sensory-organ category: the sensitivity of the spirit, the richness of the imagination and the receptivity to subtle distinctions constitute the many layers of meaning that are inborn. This is what manifests itself in the child who even in infancy does not gape dumbly at the world but visibly takes notice. This is the unmistakable mark of talent.

There are universally talented people whose abilities lie in several directions. For such people, thanks to the "plethora of riches", choosing their true calling is extremely difficult. A great weight descends on the shoulders of their instructors, for it is they who can be of most help. Much worth has gone astray as the result of an incorrect or hesitant decision.

The basis of talent, then is psychological in origin. But it is only a latent faculty, which determines a person's worth and ensures that it is possible for him to stand out in some field and achieve better than average results, in so far as physiological abilities accompany the talent. These abilities decide whether or not the talent will assert itself; insofar as they are present, the talent is a blessing in every facet of life; but insofar as they are absent, the talent will not be able to develop, and will have no room to assert and prove itself. In that case it is a curse, as talent constantly spurs one on to activity, indeed to eminent feats, for a person's spiritual disposition tells him that he is called to rise above the average. The sole task of the educator is to bring these abilities to a point where they can give expression to the talent. This is the sole task in teaching, but the one most difficult and most heavy with responsibility. To accomplish it is the teacher's greatest reward. The conditions needed to make it successful are: 1. recognizing the talent, i.e., noticing the child's exceptional features; 2. noticing which physiological strength can be brought into the teaching process, i.e. what direction his inclinations and abilities take; 3. developing, through the art of teaching, the abilities that have been recognized, in such a way that over-enthusiasms are guided in the right direction and the child's self-respect is kept alive. The child must therefore be neither spoilt nor crushed in spirit. He must be kept in a cheerful atmosphere, free from nagging, but guided with a consistently firm hand, in the knowledge and recognition of the fact that apart from our superiority in teaching methods and learning, he may well be the more talented of the two of us; 4. instruction should not be through preordained musical patterns—everything must be deduced from the music's own course; and while we are leading and guiding the child, we should try, as far as is necessary and possible, to grow towards him. We must know his exceptional characteristics, work in a manner that is appropriate to them, and make him use them in the spirit of "noblesse oblige". It is very difficult to harness a talented pupil's tendency towards excess, and very difficult to get him used to steady and systematic work. Indeed, it is difficult to get him used to anything, for his imagination is continually on the move. He is constantly discovering something new, and he is very often right. It is difficult, in the course of teaching, to adjust constantly to the situation of the moment in such a way as to make that situation help the child's development. And in the end we must realize and accept that after a time—admittedly with the help of what we have given him—he will outgrow us. After we have given him everything we know and perhaps, in the more fortunate cases, helped him towards a suitable new teacher, we shall lose him. This is the order of things; but there are many other things for us to do in teaching. We should not confuse the concept of talent with abilities, which are the manifestations of the organs of sense, and the prerequisites if talent is to blossom out. (The son of a colleague of mine, a first-rate music teacher, already had completely reliable perfect pitch at the age of 5–6. He had in every respect a very good feeling for music, and was also dexterous in his movements. He was, of course, attracted by a career in music. His father, however, took the view that all the same, he would never be a real musician because—as he said—he never saw the child moved to tears by a story, a poem, a picture, or music being so *beautiful*. His son is now an excellent engineering student, and is training to be a sound engineer. His father was right: he was very musical, but not talented, for talent belongs not to the category of the senses, but to that of the feelings—it is the sensitivity of the spirit.) So the fact that someone is musical, however much so, is still no guarantee that he is also talented; on the other hand, if someone is talented, that is still no guarantee that he is really musical. As regards artistic training, of course, the latter case is the more promising. For musicality—given that hearing, a sense of form, etc., are functions of the sense organs—can to a large degree be developed on an intellectual basis, provided the emotional richness and the yearning for music are present; but it is extremely difficult to produce emotional richness in the most musical of individuals if the appropriate spiritual make-up is not there.

What are the abilities that make it possible for a musical talent to blossom out, if they are developed into skills through practice?

a) Musicality, i.e. the factors that make up hearing,
b) concentration and perseverance (simply, the capacity for hard work),
c) ability and memory,
d) psychological and physical flexibility (dexterity).

These abilities can and must be developed to a certain extent in everyone who wants to deal with music—even in the intelligent listener. (I am referring to the earlier statement that even listening to music is not a passive action, but demands mental participation.)

Let us examine in turn the elements necessary if musical talent is to develop.

a) *Musicality*

Its constituents were amply expounded in the chapter entitled "Music".

b) *Concentration and perseverance (hard work)*

A true musical talent is the one that not only hears music extremely well, but really lives it. His imagination, like his activity, really finds expression in music. The true musician does not need to be goaded into music—for he is virtually incapable of not making music in some form or other for days on end—but his activity within it needs guiding. A young child with a real musical talent will remain quiet, motionless and really concentrate when he hears music. He will try to express himself in music very early on, with spontaneous singing or playing a toy instrument, or perhaps at the piano. This activity is a precondition of true musical talent.

Activity, however, does not equal hard work. For a child, making music is as much a game as anything else. I mentioned in an earlier chapter that children are in fact practising all day long from infancy onwards. They are instinctively, assiduously and continuously setting their developing organs to work and keeping them at work, in order to develop and get stronger as their age demands. This is one of the sources of a child's resistance, and his rebelliousness against instructions from parents and teachers, for he feels he should now be "practising" something other than what they happen to require.

Up to a point one should give way to a child's will in this direction, for if he always does everything on command, according to a time-table laid down by adults, he will become either resistant (aggressive), or uncertain and helpless.

A talented child will not practise in the way the teacher considers most advisable, either. His practice too is a game, and it only differs from the average child's in that it is a musical game. What we currently call hard work is rather, where talent is concerned, the concentration of attention and perseverance arising from persistent interest.

Goethe said that genius is hard work. Of course, not all hard work is a guarantee of talent, but it is really true that only those whose inner forces do not let them rest, and who are forever seeking after truth, are really talented. Is hard work necessarily a faithful expression of this restless endeavour? It is not certain. Talent's hard work resembles obsession rather than work at a regular tempo. It is, in fact, rather more true the other way round, and the teacher must bear this in mind. To a certain extent regular hard work can replace talent, but irregular over-exertion that arises unhealthily from obsession can have a damaging influence on a talented child's success or even ruin it. It is clear from this, too, how great is the teacher's responsibility—not to mention the damage that the excessive pushing that stems from a teacher's obsession can cause!

In determining the amount of hard work necessary one should take into account that a child, even a talented one, cannot be expected to produce a performance which has been perfected to the last detail. Attempting to force this often deadens the spontaneous expression of talent. *"Erspielen"*, the need to work a piece out to the last detail, is a rare phenomenon even among genuinely talented children. If the teacher, prompted by the talent, still demands this, it can easily turn into drilling, which does more harm than good. In many cases it will be most constructive to leave this development to time, when the pupil's own ear will require a more precise attention to detail.

c) *Reasoning ability and memory*

In order to shape the music, to follow the way the pieces have been formed, i.e. to give a meaningful performance, reasoning ability is necessary.

Here the question of the connection between the performer and the active listener crops up again. A meaningless musical performance causes much suffering to an active listener, while he will get equally as much pleasure from a logical performance as from an ardently longed-for gift. The listener may be able to follow the logic of the performance consciously, though he is more likely to feel it instinctively. A logical performance is refreshing, while one without logic is irritating or boring.

There is great need for the ability to reason in memorizing, too. We must now examine memory as a constituent of talent, and see what music teaching knows about memorizing.

Musical memory develops along the same lines as any other type of memory, and can be cultivated on the same terms. It is well known that the ability to memorize develops with practice and atrophies through lack of practice (memory for numbers, addresses, names, etc.). The mind can be trained to register things in a certain direction as the need arises with the appropriate concentration and in a chosen order. Things we consider important stick in our minds better than those we find unimportant. The brain protects itself against overburdening by throwing out, forgetting the things considered insignificant. Up to a point a prerequisite for a good memory is not to overburden the brain with superfluous memories. From this point of view the brain must be kept consciously in order. Generally speaking, a certain relentlessness is necessary for the efficient working of the brain, and one cannot afford to be sentimental. A consistently purposeful person will throw the superficial ballast out of his memory to let the important experiences take root. Memory, like abilities in general, can be cultivated with practice. It is essential to memorize and play without the score. Practice done in order to develop the memory differs from the practice of other abilities in that it is completely mechanical and can be done without bringing the intellect into play, provided the appropriate manual dexterity and instinctive musicality are there. (When other abilities are practised, the danger always arises that various mistakes will become ingrained if we play mechanically.) If this is the case, there is no need for the child to be forced into an awareness of what he is doing. Most pianists learn by heart, in this way. (During one of her courses for teachers Margit Varró* brought up the question of how different people learn a piece without the score. She then asked her students to observe and comment on their own memorizing processes. She hardly got a definite and intelligent answer. It seems that the observation of this process is such a complicated psychological operation that a music teacher who has learnt by heart all his life has neither the concentration, reasoning ability nor the strength of mind to analyse it. Someone truly talented, who really *lives* his music, clearly has no need to guide his memory. He can follow the music so surely by ear, and his playing apparatus can execute so precisely this ear's commands that he can play quite instinctively; with him, the intellect remains in the subconscious. Any kind of aid or support for the memory is superfluous here.)

As in the case of the child prodigy, the talented pupil should be the model in the method used to teach memorizing. Since, however, only intellectual means can be used for instruction, the teacher must always know what he wants, and must get beneath the talented child's consciousness.

Sándor Kovács** carried out some extremely noteworthy experiments on memorizing. Their results are quite incontrovertible. But only in the case of very musical and disciplined musicians. Memorizing purely from the score, without the instrument, is extremely practical for the highly talented (and considerate to the neighbours), but presents less musical pupils, who do not instinctively have such a highly developed ability to reason with an enormously difficult task. Here again the teacher has to divide talent's accomplishment into its constituent parts and ration them out in practical quantities, according to the degree of ability in those of average talent.

By playing the musical material to be memorized from the score, the pupil should if possible get well enough acquainted with it, to be able to anticipate each note in the process by hearing it in advance. Until this can be done, one must not attempt to play without a score. Making mistakes and then checking them later by ear is an unreliable and highly irritating type of practice. If the pupil can hear and play a piece, or part of it from the score and then anticipate

---

*Margit Picker Varró (born 1881) has enriched her piano method with numerous pedagogical principles and musical promptings, both in her teaching practice and in her books of methodology.
**Sándor Kovács (1886–1918) was a music-teacher of world-wide significance. His main principle was that the mental side of teaching should become conscious and the technical side automatic.

reliably, memorizing at a conscious level can begin by building on this: pointing out the harmonic sequences and chords in classical pieces, getting to know the individual movement of the parts in a polyphonic piece, etc. Anticipation by the ear should be followed by theoretical sureness, and on this basis the execution can take place. This is the process that goes on subconsciously in the very musical pupil. Theoretical awareness can, however, be dispensed with if we can be perfectly sure of the piece by ear.

With pupils of average ability we can rarely count on their ear and theoretical knowledge giving reliable and precise instructions to the playing mechanism. That is the fortunate case where the ear and the physical ability—to use Martienssen's word—are in prestabilized harmony. It is extremely difficult to produce this ability through teaching; awareness and memorizing without the instrument are not enough; only a great deal of practice can lead to it—if it can be made automatic at all. The breakdown of memory, which is common not only with pupils but also with concert artists, also proves that prestabilized harmony is the sort of natural gift that can hardly be compensated for by hard work. It should be pointed out that prestabilized balance is what makes up for regular practice in the case of natural amateurs; they, too, feel in their hands the music they have appropriated. It is a rare quality and an almost irreplaceable requirement for memorizing. Its disadvantage is that talented people with such abilities can hardly be habituated to any kind of conscious study or even score reading, since for them instinctive music-making is a joyful, carefree yet fruitful game, in which all work seems burdensome and superfluous. It is natural that everyone is only capable of memorizing by ear in the tonality they know well. They must have a good knowledge of the so-called style in order to hear the music with such certainty that they can then play it easily without the score. For instance, the pupils who largely work on Classical and Romantic music are virtually incapable of memorizing polyphonic or contemporary pieces by ear, however musical they are.

d) *Psychological and physical flexibility (dexterity)*

The characteristic known as dexterity is an extremely important requirement if talent is to develop. The concept of flexibility, perhaps, better combines all the constituents that are necessary for the development of a good pianist. Flexibility means not only the ability to move quickly but also the capacity for adapting quickly, too—not just in terms of movement, but also in hearing and thought. A pianist of dexterity, for example, may be able to play extremely quickly; but in order for this rapidity to produce the appropriate sound flexible adaption is needed, not just in the movements but in hearing and in thought, within the shaping of the music. A fast passage in a Scarlatti sonata requires a totally different dexterity from one in a Bach cadenza or a Chopin nocturne. Dexterity and the ability to adapt quickly are largely a question of make-up, though they can be developed up to a point. A pupil, however, whose physique puts a strain on his playing mechanism, or whose slow reactions hinder the development of prestabilized harmony will find it very difficult to become a good pianist. In the same way, for instance, someone whose physique impedes the development of chest resonance cannot become a real singer, even with the most expert vocal training.

The question of fast tempi naturally comes into the category of dexterity, too. But it should not be thought that speed depends exclusively on dexterity. The tempo can only be increased when, apart from mechanical dexterity, the tone and the appropriation of the material have reached a stage where they do not require attention, i.e. that they have become automatic. (He can do it in his sleep, people say.)

Up to a point, tempo generally does not depend mainly on the state of one's technique at the time, but on how far one has made the piece part of oneself, and how much one is able to imagine it by anticipation. A deliberate and forced increase in tempo will either not succeed (the tempo slips back), or else prove its own undoing—the playing apparatus will stiffen up. In the course of the appropriate study and practice—if one knows the piece well—the tempo will increase by itself to the extent conceived beforehand.

4 Imagination

Perhaps there is no real need to emphasize the importance of the role played by imagination in music-making.

Traditional music teaching considered imagination, imaginative power, as belonging to the emotions. Though conception, "pre-conception"—apart from its emotional content—belongs organically to music-making, too. Conceptions may be more or less colourful and interesting according to talent and the degree of emotional richness, but a possible expression of emotion cannot compensate for a conception that suits the nature of a piece of music, especially the one that has been studied. Musical conception does not mean wayward and haphazard fantasizing. In its pedagogical sense, this conception is highly systematic and unfailingly *precedes* playing, being part of the learning of the piece. How much a given performance may be inspired by the situation of the moment, the performer's state of being, how he feels, is another matter. The importance of this and its right to exist over and above what has consciously been conceived cannot be denied. How one feels, however, can not only assist a performance and put one "on form", it can also—in the case of stage-fright—go a long way to ruining the result. If, however, what was preconceived takes place as one practises, is consciously imbibed and becomes automatic, then a poor state of being will not rule out an acceptable performance.

This, however, is only one side of imagination and conception. The other is what Martienssen—following Vaihinger—calls "fiction". That is, the transfer of imagination when the musical sound is so definitely present in the conception of the player that he is even able to realize it in his playing when the mechanics of the piano make it physically incapable of producing that sound. The player plays the instrument "as if" it could reproduce his conception. We are well aware how restricted the physical possibilities for tone colour on a piano are. A strong and definite musical conception, however, can exert such a strong influence on the mechanism of the body and the mind's will to transfer, that the piano is capable of inconceivable resonances. We cannot expect the music teacher to know about all the elements, both anatomically and acoustically, that are necessary for the correct musical solution, and we can expect this even less of the pupil. If this were our ambition, music lessons would be ground down by endless analysis which in the end would stifle musical conception. The piece simply needs to be properly conceived, and then the two mechanisms—the player's and the piano's—will function "as if" everything were possible in the most natural way. Martienssen calls this apparent possibility irrational for the sake of simplicity, though this is not the case.

Artistic solutions are not superhuman and incomprehensible, but it is not teaching's task to follow up everything to its ultimate conclusion. What would be the point? Based on the "as if" theory, an artistic conception founded on intelligence can do virtually everything. "Virtually" and "as if". Because music-making and piano teaching are not sciences—nor should they want to be—but arts. Fiction.

V THE ETHICAL SIDE OF MUSIC TEACHING

For anyone concerned with music, its human essence has a calming influence on their state of being. This is a result of its ethical content, in so far as psychological equilibrium can only come about where a certain ethical presence is apparent. The feeling of equilibrium has a calming influence, being the unconscious identification with true form, and at the same time enabling the beauty of the sound to resonate. Over-contrivance, exaggeration, insincerity and casualness do not tend towards psychical equilibrium, on the contrary: they are disturbing, upsetting and disquieting.

1 Teaching and the human aspect

How can the teacher acquire the sort of teaching technique that tends towards the human aspect?

As I mentioned in the Preface, artistic instruction is not an end in itself, but one of the means through which a culture centred on the human being can evolve. Instead of empty amusement and mental relaxation, music teaching should set its sights on psychological recuperation, a worthy use of free time, and a delight in something that contributes to the essence of life. This is true for all who are learning but just how much more important this human-centred character forming is for those who are training for a career in music hardly needs extra proof, for it is they who will turn the above aims into reality.

We have dealt amply with the special peculiarities of children in an earlier chapter. These peculiarities, and countless others that were not mentioned which will be noticed by the child's family, acquaintances and teachers, must be given considerable attention in the teaching of music. Although, after a longer period of teaching, a teacher will be capable of organizing his experiences and drawing conclusions from them in such a way as to make the listing and labelling of them a matter of routine, we still have to admit that experience is an extremely useful and indeed indispensable prerequisite for good teaching. There is no written or oral wisdom that could replace it. G. B. Shaw, always young in mind, was right when he stated that it is not the amount of experience that makes a person experienced but the capacity for it. A talented and thoughtful young man can acquire more useful experience in a few years than a bureaucrat is capable of producing in his whole life. The first thing in making use of one's experiences is not to lose sight of one's aim, which is always the service of musical culture through instruction. To put it in a stock phrase that is true, but has been worn to a commonplace: "We are building socialism with musical culture." It is true; and we may only build with the most cultured and most human means. The objectives can and must be classified and perhaps graded, their execution programmed and divided up; but one thing is quite inadmissible—cheapening them. In every single case the ultimate aim is to raise the pupil to a higher cultural level. How and to what extent this can be achieved depends on his or her personality, the circumstances, and many other factors. Since no two pupils are alike, and every year, every hour and every moment is different, offering different possibilities and revealing different impossibilities, no recipe can be given. Pedagogical experiences may only be applied through the filter of the pupil and the circumstances. What for one person is a joy and a blessing is an intolerable bore and curse for another.

For this reason it should be made clear that we cannot provide an infallible formula for the teacher-to-be or the practising teacher on a refresher course on how something should be taught.

The teacher must be made acquainted with the subject, but he must work out for himself in each case how it should be passed on; this cannot be expressed in laws of eternal validity. We cannot, for instance, explain how pupils should be taught to shape the music. We can make the teacher himself understand how to become aware of the music's content and of the way this content is expressed in the music's form, and if we succeed he will be able to follow in its path, and will also be able to pass it on to his pupils. Modern music for example, does not need to be explained; rather, the teacher should listen to, and *play,* a lot of modern music in order to assimilate its melodic world and system of construction. He will soon be able to distinguish which is good and which is not, and will then be able to teach it.

The teacher-to-be should get to know the music and the child and then himself *develop the proper connection between them in the name of human values and morality*. Personal tricks can be devised in a moment of inspiration; but to copy these or any kind of personal habit without conviction and concoct a teaching method out of them for one's own use is not ethical. Of course it can happen that we benefit from copying some personal device—trick. (If only by winning the appreciation of the person we have copied it from.)

We should not, however, go to the other extreme either; a great deal can be learnt from good books and good musicians, and insight can be acquired that we might never have discovered by ourselves. This can sometimes include such devices too, but these will only become a substantial plus if we bolster what we have learnt with our own observations and reinforce them with our own experiences. We should not copy them but filter them through our own convictions and thereby *appropriate them and make them our own*. This belongs to the ethics of teaching, for this is how we must pass on our experiences and knowledge to our pupils: with conviction and convincingly. Those who learn slavishly and collect other people's experiences, who do not themselves evolve and go on evolving, developing and updating their own teaching methods year by year, will never teach creatively, and will force their pupils to imitate slavishly as well.

There is not a single work by an expert pedagogue that can absolve the practising teacher from constant research, continuous experiment, and, most emphatically, from practising his own playing, in which his knowledge and musical character will be constantly renewed. If he does not rediscover music again and again as he plays the piano, if he is not for ever finding new musical and technical solutions, his teaching will get increasingly bureaucratic. The same thing cannot be done the same way twice over: the second solution will either be better, perfecting itself through practice and experiment, or else it will mechanically remain the same, that is, it will be worse than the previous one. A very great deal can be learnt from other people, but only the things we ourselves develop from what we have learnt, through self-education, are of real value.

Copied knowledge is as worthless and unpleasant as feigned emotions.

The pupil should not be taught but should be led into a proper attitude towards music, so that his critical sense will develop in such a way that he himself will find the right way as soon as possible. The teacher's greatest achievement is when he becomes superfluous, and when the pupil arrives at the correct musical solution without his help. Indeed, the teacher's greatest joy is when his former pupil surpasses him and when the teacher with a permanent desire to develop can ask musical advice of his pupil. This is a natural development and the proof of good teaching.

2 Inflexible music teaching

Ever since learning to play the piano became more widespread, more fashionable, so to speak—with the onset of bourgeois civilization—attempts have been made to deal with piano teaching in a more general way. It was, you might say, the golden age of music when the only people who learnt music were those who were in a musical environment from birth onwards. As they grew up, they hung around great masters, either as members of the family or as musical assistants, and imbibed music on every available instrument.

In later times, however, they no longer studied as musical apprentices, and did not learn from the masters: bourgeois culture brought with it the obligatory and socially requisite piano-playing of young ladies. The latter were taught by music teachers or later by piano mistresses who had become dulled, embittered and withered under the influence of many untalented pupils and their vain, demanding parents, and were duly paid the price of their soulless and half-hearted labours. The piano-playing fashion did not give much joy (of course there were always exceptions), so some means had to be found of giving a more meaningful form to the mass teaching that was taking the place of the old amateurism. Fortunately something always turns up at times like this. Conscientious teachers appeared on the scene who tried to systematize and re-interpret the old musical freedom, and put a brake on the uninhibited, senseless chaos that had recently come about. The caste of the methodical teacher came into being, and despite many blunders it created something that had some sense in mass teaching even for pupils with no musical inclination. Great mistakes were made, but so, too, were great discoveries, as physicists, anatomists and psychologists joined forces with musicians. Music teaching gained in standing, because it was being taken seriously by exceptional people. Good and bad schools, useful and harmful methods came into being, and at both the artistic and mass educational level the standard rose, even if in a spiralling or zigzag fashion.

The birth and development of music teaching were accompanied by many mistakes and difficulties—as are most births and developments in the life of humanity. Initiating the mass of averagely talented people into the study of music brought about a more general interest in music, and—since the mass of average teachers were similarly of moderate ability—led to a widening of musical interest. However, at the same time, indeed, as a consequence of this widespread interest, there occurred much trivial music-making which led to the domination of the worst kind of dilettantism. For teaching by method, rules had to be created, in fact hammered out, that everyone could memorize; and to this end the model teaching pieces had to be written, and in many cases thrown together. Now there was no Anna Magdalena Bach collecting music for the use of children with her own refined taste and with the help of the king of composer-teachers, J. S. Bach. There were only pedantic Piano Tutors rampant the world over, devoid of music but rich in commonplaces. The closer these tutors were to the rules, and the further away they were from true, intuitive, polysemantic music, the greater was their success and sphere of influence. Drawing up rules took precedence over music. The teachers of the great virtuosi, who gained distinction in developing virtuosity, finally gave the *coup de grâce* to mass teaching. Polysemantic, truly artistic music disappeared almost entirely from the agenda in popular teaching. Disgusted with the dryness of music-teaching—or to put it better, rule encapsulated technique-teaching—many people sought solace in music's emotional content. This resulted in the natural tendency of teachers and pupils of average ability to set off the dry technique with emotional, so-called musical demands. These "musical" demands, however, did not stem from the music's inner laws but from external, imposed, and usually pictorial associations. The pieces that proved particularly suitable for this were the various character-pieces with appropriate illustrations. Of course I am not thinking of Schumann's Album for the Young or Debussy's Children's Corner, not of pieces for children by the great masters, but of their imitators, who lived off them and served the mass audience.

It is a well-known fact that the greatest masters of Romantic music themselves generally used pictorial and literary associations in their works. Such highly-charged and genuinely artistic manifestations, however, are naturally not applicable in music for children, and it is not even true that they inspire children to play better. An irresolute music teacher, not knowing what to do with the child or the music, resorts to pictures and comparisons, in order to be doing something. A talented child's imagination, however, does not insist on assistance of this kind, and an untalented one will not even be musically inspired by it. Of course, Liszt, too, used pictures like this, as his famous saying on the second movement of the Moonlight Sonata demonstrates: "A single flower between two rocks." This is a very beautiful poetic expression; but no one has ever played the sonata the better for it.

In Hungary, too, there were great teachers who did much to promote piano teaching, but sometimes went too far and caused harm as well. It does not fall within the framework of this book to pass judgment on their work, but it is impossible not to refer to one marvellous teacher, who was an incomparable representative of the ethic that has been so far outlined: Leó Weiner*. He did not talk about flowers and rocks and storms but showed everything that needed to be shown with his pedal and fingering indications. He demonstrated rather than explained; his behaviour was neither pompous nor reverential nor especially dynamic: his passion fired enthusiasm through his unparalleled conscientiousness and honesty. He did not demand a lot, but "everything". He knew no compromise, there was no detail that could be passed over. Yet he was not a pedant. How could this be? Because with him insistence on details arose from a single dialectic unity: the totality of the work. He never said this, but anyone who followed his teaching attentively necessarily felt it. The expressions he used were not scientifically based but intuitive, for example:

*Leó Weiner (1885-1960), composer, worked as a piano teacher at the Budapest Academy of Music. He taught primarily chamber music, but the musical atmosphere that radiated from him affected everyone who came near him. Numerous books and transcriptions of his have been published.

"this should be done with a collapsing wrist" or "you must lean into that note". He wrote no methodology, nor even a pedagogical study. I once asked him why he did not write about correct pedalling, since he was so sure in his approach. He answered that things like that cannot be written about. It was simply a matter of "using the pedals properly". He was the mortal enemy of any sort of written formulation of inflexible rules in practical music teaching. He knew exactly how and why something should be performed this way or that, but the only concrete answer he gave was, "This is what Beethoven demands". He, who was precision personified, knew very well that it is impossible to set down in writing with a clear conscience the things that are prompted by the teacher's inspiration with a particular pupil at a particular moment in a particular place.

3 The formation of a work ethic

Let us risk applying a few general principles to music teaching in connection with the relationship between teacher and pupil. Principles, I should point out, not rules and certainly not laws.

After laying the foundations of the pupil's relationship to music, perhaps the next most important task is to establish a work ethic.

Given the way the pupil is overburdened at school, this can only be accomplished by methods diametrically opposed to those of the past. We are talking about practice, of course.

Children studying music in the past and those of the present have in common that they would rather play than work. So to begin with we should try to distinguish the difference that generally exists between work and play.

It is commonly said that child's play is also work. This is not entirely true. There are two types of playing: one is really a preparation for practical development and work, and can almost be called systematic; it was through realizing this that I dared to state, in the chapter on the Child, that children virtually practise all day long. The essential feature of the other type of play is that it is completely unrestrained, and free of any responsibilities—it is purely the product of the child's imagination. The first kind of play, even if it is not conscious and systematic, does have an aim. The only thing the second kind has in common with real life is that it may draw on it. The appearance of these two kinds of play is an indication of life in every child; the proportion and intensity with which they appear will depend largely on the inclinations he is born with, but influences undergone in his infancy and even before birth also play a part. A more detailed breakdown, exposition and pursuit of this question is not the task of the teacher—or parent—but of the appropriate science.

Generally it is better, and more fruitful, for the teacher to go deeply into practical observations rather than science. "It has been proved", or "experiments have shown"—graphs, numerical data and elaborate tests are very often misleading, for real life simply will not let itself be put into compartments. People who deal professionally with life rather than science often misinterpret science's results, misapply them, and run even greater risks if they develop them further and approach practical matters from a scientific point of view. I do not want to put a teacher's work before that of a scientist, but it is better for science to draw its conclusions from practice than for us to try to make scientific observations valid at all costs. As we are not experts in the branch of science concerned, we may make serious errors of understanding, and it is always the child who suffers as a result.

The two kinds of play must be observed as early on and as closely as possible, for it will emerge from this—with greater or lesser certainty—whether the child will be the thoughtful, methodical, so-called hard-working type during his studies, or rather the dreamy, fantasizing type. In talented children the two types may, of course, blend together in happy proportions.

This tendency, which shows itself in play, is of decisive importance for the whole of life, and education can do the most harm by not taking it into consideration. The teacher may, for example, not be able to fit the child into his own ideal, and tries instead to force his own method of study on the pupil. This is the greatest crime he can commit. Getting the child used to working and developing a work ethic can only be achieved in accordance with the type of play involved.

In the first years of teaching, a teacher usually has an easier time with the child who is the practising type. In this case he has only to concern himself with establishing a good relationship. A pupil of the dreamy, musing type needs much more patience and understanding, and in fact, to begin with, it is virtually impossible to get him used to serious, regular work. These are the type who teach themselves, who only learn from their own experiences, and only achieve their ends through self-criticism. But it is they who are often of greater worth.

What can be achieved in the longer term through traditional educational means: scolding, persuasion, punishment?

Nothing.

It would, of course, be a mistake to praise without conviction and overlook mistakes out of misconceived pedagogical aims. Sometimes we must speak our minds very firmly, but this should be brief, decisive and to the point, and not in the form of nagging or preaching.

What is useful and important is to inspire self-confidence and develop healthy self-esteem. The pupil must feel we have confidence in him and do not demand more of him than he is capable of. Gradualness, consistency, confidence, and optimistic, happy atmosphere are the necessary prerequisites to the formation of a good relationship. Demands that are too high and inconsistent, and behaviour that is callous, nagging, impatient or disparaging can make work painful and, after a time, impossible, for both teacher and pupil. I do not subscribe to the widely-held and attractive-sounding axiom that there are no unteachable pupils, only bad teachers. Countless other elements besides the music teacher influence a child and can make studying music impossible. There are unteachable children, but there are so few of them that they can be passed over when teaching methods are being worked out. There is one further psychological factor in this connection to be taken into account, which is nearly as rare as the one just mentioned; it is that ineradicable antagonism can exist in the personalities of the teacher and the pupil. This stems not from the child's character but from his upbringing, which the teacher is powerless to overcome. This fact can arouse mutual and insurmountable antipathy on both sides.

Finally, a word on parental involvement. In my view, a good foundation for the teacher–pupil relationship is assured if parents (or grandparents) have no part in it. The parents' only positive role should be to ensure conditions for practice and attending lessons. Given the arguments already put forward, it would perhaps be superfluous to emphasize that parental vanity, strictness, and methods based on rewards and punishments can only harm the way the pupil evolves in musical and human terms. The child's development, too, must be creative, and here the parents' natural bias, important in other respects, does not help. Parental help—even when the parent is a music teacher—can only produce results in specific instances: intensive training for a performance for example, which is very often harmful to gradual development. The prospect of regular rewards and punishments can do much to ruin the formation of a work ethic if it is adhered to, and still more if it is not. This, of course, is not a law that admits no exception. Here, too, rigid rules do more harm than occasional relaxations, or even mistakes.

VI THE QUESTION OF "STYLE"

1 Definition of terms

"The only worthwhile performance of music written in a style of the past is the one which is based on the musical practice of today. Everything else is merely the *imitation of a tradition,* which we do not 'inherit' in the accepted sense of the word, but essentially *re-create*." (Stravinsky)

In music teaching a number of expressions feature as technical terms and are used magisterially and often misused without any explanation being given of their true meaning. "Style" is one of them. The word derives from the Latin name for a pointed writing instrument, a *stilus*. Its figurative meaning was generalized, and was and is used to this day in its original form in connection with virtually every art.

But what essentially does this word mean in the figurative sense, in which it is used?

Mode of expression. Modes of expression relate primarily to the written and spoken word, and both originally and in their later use have been applied mainly to characterizing modes of speaking and writing. And although the characteristic of style has been taken over into the other branches of the arts, it has nonetheless kept its sense most convincingly and most expressively in literature.

Its definition with regard to music is not so clear-cut. Musicology may be content with its variety of meanings, but in music teaching the fact that the expression "style" covers many things is troublesome.

Musicology classifies styles according to periods. But the ways in which the word is applied are arbitrary and confused. And if we add that often we do not refer to style as music's outward form according to its period, but say: Bach's style, Beethoven's style, etc., and rightly so, since the more significant composers had their own individual character within the style of the period, then what should we call style in teaching? We are clearly dealing with a definition so inexact that it merely serves to spare the teacher the trouble of looking for his own solutions. The musical and technical solutions to pieces are explained by using the term style which is extremely convenient, as it conceals irresponsibility beneath an appearance of precision. If we know what is prescribed by the "style" of a work, then the mode of performance (rhythm, agogics, phrasing), the touch, and so on, are given accordingly. This, for instance, would be the explanation of baroque music: an austere mode of performance, without any great legatos, variations of tempo or cantabiles. And for Romantic music: emotional playing with free tempo, a lot of pedal, etc. Often even general musical questions are approached from the point of view of style. Stereotypes have always been popular in teaching.

Things get a bit complicated if, for example, we talk not about the classical style generally, but about Mozart's style in particular. Though in such cases the requirements for the widely-accepted Mozart stereotypes will be to hand.

So what is it all about? What sort of impenetrable mass does the musical treasure-chest marked "style" conceal? Clearly, the word does not have the precise meaning that is ascribed to it in common parlance. Yet the precise use of expressions and an educated terminology are much more important factors in teaching than the amount of care devoted to them by pedagogy would indicate. We must clarify the concept itself, and only thereafter can we move on to a clarification of the various characteristics.

Style comprises two completely distinct concepts, and can accordingly be used in two senses that must be distinguished from each other: style is

a) the technique of the mode of expression appropriate to a given period, and

b) the particular mode of expression of the artist, the way he interprets what he has to impart through a selection of technical means.

The two concepts clearly have an impact on each other, in so far as the spirit of the age undeniably affects the artist.

In one sense, then, style is a technical concept, in the other a psychological one.

Style as the technique of a mode of expression is intelligible, definable, explainable and teachable. Baroque, classical and other styles are in close connection with the taste, demands and ideology of the period, and these had an irresistible influence on both creative and performing artist. This, for the most part, is well known. Style as the mode of expression of a personality is a much more complex concept. The personality of a creative artist is much more difficult to explain than his age. What can be deduced from this as far as the practice of teaching the art of performance is concerned? Is it that the more we study the period, on the one hand, and the creative artist's personality, on the other, the more we elaborate our theories about them and the closer we stick to these in our teaching, the more reliable our teaching of style will be?

This concept is in direct opposition to the spirit of creative musical teaching. Even in its most intelligent and artistic form it leads towards stereotypes, and if not perhaps in its original form, in the hands of a true artist-teacher, then most definitely as applied by those who try to imitate him.

2 Stylistic constraint, stylistic confusion

Style as the technical realization of a musical idea is a fairly concrete concept. The rules governing it can be precisely formulated and taught. This, however, is for use in the teaching of artistic creation (composition). In a good school of composition, the pupils should get acquainted with every style to the extent of being able to construct something within its technical framework. This is a stylistic exercise, and its aim is the acquisition of a many-sided technique. It is self-evident, however, that a composer's true identity will only come to the fore in the style evolved by the age he lives in, for the age influences not only the technique but also him as a person. However skilfully and inventively he may write in the stylistic technique of yesterday or the day before, his invention will not be convincing.

In former times there was hardly any difference between creative and performing artists in respect of style, for only contemporary music was played, and that usually by the composers. But ever since the music of different periods has played an equal part in musical life, the tasks facing performers, and also teachers, have been much more complex. What the student performer has to accomplish in the course of his studies today makes demands that are virtually impossible to fulfil. And very few people fulfil them. The stylistic demands are narrowed down, and the average pupil's potential reaches its upper limit in the interpretation of the Classical and Romantic styles, while the remainder merely features as set study-material. There is neither time, love nor conviction left for going deeply into masterpieces that are less spectacular on the concert platform.

The performing artist, however, can choose freely from the styles, and although nearly everyone's main aim is to be outstanding in every style, he may decide to specialize in one of them. In practice, of course, this cannot be achieved. The artist's psychological and physical make-up cannot, in equal measure, be suitable for every variety of style. This is not contradicted by the fact that there are pianists whose performances are convincing whatever they play, since, disregarding the style's accepted hallmarks, they make such good use of the absolute laws governing music that they satisfy both the listener's sense of form and his craving for experience in the highest degree. Only performers who can assimilate music through both their talent and their knowledge and then project it in performance are capable of this. By contrast, there are many highly gifted performers who would do better to specialize (on the podium at least, if not when they practise) in certain kinds of music that suit their personality and physical attributes. In this way they may achieve perfection instead of trying to prove their suitability for everything in Sisyphus-like labours, endangering their self-confidence and boring the audience.

For piano teaching, however, the fact that these days every style simultaneously plays a part in musical life presents a virtually insoluble problem. Music teachers cannot allow themselves to be selective even when they recognize that a pupil has an inclination and a capacity for certain styles. To encourage the narrowing of the performing artist's style is not even permissible when the pupil's inclinations are obvious, and far less so when the teacher moves towards the point of least resistance in accordance with his own inclinations.

Should we begin by examining to what extent a narrowing of style is harmful and to what extent inevitable; to what extent it can be blamed on teaching, and to what extent its opposite could be put to good use? I believe we would come nearer the solution by deciding correctly on orders of sequence and priority, clearing up confusion, setting out clear aims and ignoring stereotypes and irrelevancies.

Why did we say that the simultaneous presence of the different styles in our musical life set teaching an impossible task? Because a good music teacher will not be satisfied if his pupil completes the curriculum satisfactorily and plays the set pieces in different styles. Learning to play these pieces will only be meaningful if the pupil derives some musical benefit from them, i.e. if they stamp an ineradicable musical experience on him. Only then will he be spiritually and emotionally enriched. Is this conceivable within a style whose world of sound is foreign to him?

3 Teaching the various styles

The various styles should be introduced into teaching in a certain order and within a certain period, leaving time for the pupil to come to terms with their world of sound and feel at home there. He should learn to feel that their logic is natural and to accept their tonality and idiom along with their dissonances and resolutions. Let us look at a possible, a conceivable order, during which the pupil would go through the various styles from the point where he starts to learn the piano up to his final training. This order would not be chronological; it would be in line with the human development of the child and the young person.

The beginning can be nothing other than the ambiance of children's songs. This is the most direct route from play to work based on the pupils' demands in terms of sound. The primitive way in which children's song are shaped is unambiguous. They provide sufficient material for the basic elements to be assimilated. They should be the material with which the pupil actively experiences the formal elements of statement and answer, and the most basic divisions and interconnections. Following on from this he will recognize the regular beat and the rhythmic values that divide it, and will get a feeling for primitive tonality. Alongside this melodic development, we should exploit and further develop the child's demands in terms of movement with little games, exercises and snippets of music composed for the purpose. A child's demands in terms of sound are much more colourful and many-sided than an adult's, in whom the sound-world of one particular style has taken root. Musical stereotypes are still foreign to him, so things which differ from them are not wrong to his ears. The possibility exists to direct his demands in terms of sound towards a richer tonality than the heptatonic. He can be made accustomed to accept the music of today through play, with no difficulty at all. Here, of course, appropriate little pieces are necessary, which provide through their more varied pitch opportunities for movement. Exercises, melodies and chordal fragments from modern music prepared to this end would be the most suitable here. We cannot expect the child to concentrate on form or harmony, but we can expect him to be inventive and understanding in play. Therefore, following children's songs and alongside them, a basis can be created for the atmosphere of today's style. This requires at least two years, if we are aiming at education in a feeling for style and even then it will only be successful if we do not mix in other styles during the two years. The exercises and fragments of melody and chords found in the music of today find their immediate follow-up in baroque music. The sound-world of Viennese classicism would cause an interruption in this process. The little exercises mentioned above, of course, mould the music mainly in sequences, imitations and variations, and insofar as chords are sounded, they do not follow the system based on thirds. So with their Janus-like faces they look partly towards Bartókian and partly towards polyphonic music.

Bach put the crowning touch to a fully matured style in polyphony and in baroque forms; he did not go looking for the necessary means, but imbued the already well-tried existing ones with the inventiveness that flowed from his talent; his music differs from that of his contemporaries only in that it is exceptionally varied and polysemantic. This is why it causes such difficulties in teaching. Bach is never primitive and even less stereotyped: the means he uses are well-tried and represent the high-point of a style, and are at the same time extremely rich. Bartók was born into the Romantic and Post-Romantic styles and indeed began his career by carrying them on. But once he came to know the simplicity of folk music, he became almost disgusted with the luxuriance of the bourgeois styles, the quest for sonority for its own sake, and the emotional excess of musical art. His puritan artistic disposition inclined him towards the simple and intelligible. But since he was separated by centuries from baroque music and its technique—and so much had happened in between—he had to seek and create a new kind of simplicity. He could not use Bach's richness, and when, as a creative artist at one with his time and committed to the service of progress, he sought the nobly simple, he could not turn into an imitator of the baroque, but had to create a simplicity which would divest itself of overblown romanticism in the same way as the masters of preclassicism had unambiguously broken with the over-complicated polyphonic style. Bartókian simplicity does not suffer its melodic shaping and part-writing to be slipshod. Bartók sought simplicity and austerity in his new style, in his composer's ars poetica, the *Mikrokosmos,* and this is why this music is the best suited to lead to a knowledge, an understanding of the noblest of all music—to Bach, who, in spirit, was just as austere and simple as Bartók. If we come to know Bach through Bartók, we shall stay in the present while being enriched by the best traditions of the past.

This curriculum is quite different from present-day practice, which situates Classical major-minor tonality at the centre of teaching for beginners. We must go into the reasons for this more fully.

It is a widely-held view in piano teaching that learning music should begin according to physiological logic, i.e. in the order of harmonics. In teaching beginners, Viennese classical music's dominance is sustained by the principle that the harmonic order is best suited if we start with the simplest harmonies and work towards the more complicated ones. The major triad is situated at the very beginning of the harmonic scale, and is thus derived from nature. This argument, however, with its "scientific" support tells its own tale—that we only want to think in harmonies! It is true that in harmonic terms, the chords of the ninth and the fourth, etc., are more difficult to hear than major and minor ones—but why should we inevitably and unassailably start the listening process with chords?

Considering that learning to play the piano became widespread at a time when classical harmonies were predominant in musical practice, it is not surprising that piano teaching followed their course: the aim both for beginners and for the advanced pupils was playing classically harmonized music. Life, however, has left this practice behind, and today such music is no longer modern. Even though the Classical Viennese masters still occupy a pre-eminent position in musical practice today, their hegemony is shared by the music that comes before and after them. Piano teaching, too, must take note of this. Teachers with a tendency towards conservatism make reference in their counter-arguments to the progressivity that lays down the law of consonance according to the law of harmonics. They refer to music's development and insist on the development of a child's hearing following this law, although as music developed, monophonic melodies were followed by polyphony, where consonance and dissonance asserted themselves differently from the way they did in classically harmonized music.

If we examine the vertical relationship between the parts in pure polyphony, thoroughly complex harmonies emerge in the parts of the polyphonic masters that are very far removed from the world of classical harmony. Even if we insist on chronological order, the search for fundamentals in simple harmonies is not justified. Moreover, it is an empirical fact, that the harmonic sense of a six to eight year-old child is not given by nature, but cultivated by teaching music of a classical nature.

According to my plan, the time for getting thoroughly acquainted with classically harmonized music would come after the tonal grounding of the first years, with its corresponding wide area of movement and a cognizance of two-part writing. Also the child will be sufficiently developed intellectually not to approach music simply as a game, but to follow what he is playing on a theoretical basis, too. Preclassical and classical pieces can be supported by the theory and practice of scales, trials and four-part chords. At this level, and meaningfully connected to the pieces being played, this practice will not be such a torture as it was in the first years, when it was a compulsory pattern quite divorced from the music. What follows next does not differ from former practice. Czerny and the great classics can come now. (Technical analysis belongs to the material for the next chapter.) At this stage, a good average pupil will already be sufficiently mature for this in terms of his sense of form, motoric skill and ability to concentrate. And after as thorough and extensive a working as possible of the classical masters (mainly Haydn!), romantic music may follow when the child is old enough. And so on.

Once the musical trend (Bartók–Bach) that follows present-day tonality and part-writing has taken root, and is followed by all the beauties and laws of classical music, there will be no need to fear playing different styles over the same period, as everything will have played its part in the appropriate place during teaching. Once the teacher has played his part, everyone can choose from among the different styles according to his own taste and inclinations.

However, neither the teacher nor the prospective artist selecting a style should neglect the fact that in what I have written above, style was only being considered as "the technique of a mode of expression appropriate to the age". In times past, a new trend buried the old one. The process began which has gained increasingly in strength up to the present day, whereby the public and many of the experts are not satisfied by the music of their contemporaries and reach back into the past in search of the characteristics of styles that were lost in oblivion. This has the effect of producing extremely complicated problems. On the positive side, first, the values of the past come to the surface once more; and since only the real values from the past are resurrected, their content in human terms is of great value to those interested in music. And secondly, by reaching back to sources (for in musical output nothing is totally new), one thing builds on another and music renews itself through tradition. The negative impact of keeping the representatives of the great styles on the programme lies in the fact that it turns music-lovers, and indeed performers, away from the present and from its new searchings and developments; they prefer to satisfy their musical needs from the past. New struggles are made more difficult because time has not yet been able to do the necessary weeding-out among those who are seeking new paths. A mixture of better and poorer compositions come before the public, and another influential factor is that audiences would rather go to what they are sure of than pick something from music that is foreign to them. Active musicians are therefore not urged on in their search for the right path either by the friendly society of inspiring performers who support them or by the great public and by prompting from their fans. Wide-ranging and thorough participation by professional critics is meagre, while participation by the public—positive or negative, in its standpoint, but at all events interested and stimulating—is virtually nil.

Can we in fact measure the impact of this?

In an atmosphere such as this, it is very difficult for the new "style" to evolve.

In this form, however, this problem is not the concern of the practising teacher.

4 Teachers, performers and style

Since—admittedly on a basis of reflection and teaching experience alone—I am constantly offering the reader a certain order that tries to present the question of style from the aspect of stylistic technique in teaching, I ought to examine what of all this can and should be taught.

It should be underlined that neither the teaching of how music is formed nor the execution of rhythm and agogics or even keyboard technique can be accomplished by observing and explaining the piece's style. The other side of the definition of style is "the artist's own mode of expression, the way he interprets what he has to say through a selection of technical means", and in spite of the strongest exertions towards a return to the past, the new demands in taste of the man of today will inevitably predominate, and a renaissance of whatever kind can be conceived in a spiral-like development. In creative art, several styles, belonging to essentially different periods, are inconceivable. It is not a contradiction that in reproductive art (performance) the music of different periods is present at the same time. But this cannot be conceived otherwise than as the reflection of the total influence of the present age. The performer creates by interpreting a work created 100–200 years ago in a different way from its composer at that time. Every age has its style of performance, and this is valid for old music too. Haven't we all felt, when listening to a few surviving records of great performers of the past, that this is not exactly what we got so enthusiastic about in the past? The young people of today do not experience the amazing impact they made on the music-lovers of the past either. Haven't we all heard comments to the effect that Bartók did not play his own works as well as today's great performers? Yet as a performer Bartók was unsurpassable of his kind, and really knew how to make his works sound. Or Huberman, one of the greatest violinists the world has seen; are his surviving records entirely satisfying? Can the musical solution that was convincing 200, 100 or even 50 years ago be adopted today? Should it be? I am convinced that this would be one of the greatest misunderstandings possible in the search for artistic truth. An age, and within it the mentality, the tempo of life, the mental and indeed physical make-up of mankind is in a constant state of change. Neither can the way art manifests itself be enclosed within the confines of past ages. The art of performance manages to give equal value to the music of the different periods because the performer's style can make any work a work of today. The reproductive artist, in his musical conception, is representative of his age in the same way as the composer. Martienssen confirms this too when he comments: "the majority of great pianists have the power to transform works ill-suited to their temperament in such a manner that they actually come into accord with the piece through their personal reproductive creative demands in terms of sound."

A few examples: Richter's Chopin is defined by his own personality, fascinating as Richter but not Chopinesque. Schumann's style, ecstatic in content, is very close to Richter. Horowitz's Chopin is titanic yet all the same true Chopin in its content. And what about Landowska's Bach, different from everyone else's and rapturously convincing? What lesson can the teacher draw from this? Performers' varying solutions for all kinds of music can be equally good and convincing provided they play with conviction according to their own personalities and the age they live in. The laws governing the music exert their own influence over and above stylistic technique. To all this we should add Martienssen's statement: "In piano teaching respect for spiritual development must stand well above the requirements and abuses of the *present*." The teacher must allow the music and the individual personality to find their legitimate expression. Rules cannot be made under the pretext of stylistic teaching that Bach, for instance, is played drily and non-legato, Chopin grandiloquently, or Bartók with angry pounding. Style as a means of expression binds only the creative artist; the recreative artist must play every work in the way the music's form, the spirit of his age and his own artistic conviction dictate. There is also no special Bach, Mozart, Chopin or Bartók touch. In every single piece by every single composer there is only what the music there demands. Of course, finding the appropriate solution to this in every case is much harder than imprinting a stylistic stamp on it. And what is more, it is not primarily touch that determines the correct solution for a work but rather its special rhythm, agogics, articulation, etc.

Style as "the expression of inner content" is often a contradiction to style as "the technique of a mode of expression". We have spoken in some detail of the affinity between the music of Bartók and Bach. Austerity, the absence of superfluous elements, an almost prudish restraint in the mode of expression, together with great variety and the polysemantism of surprising harmonic turns. But how much closer to the technique of Bach's style is that of Handel's or of Telemann's? In terms of inner content the difference between them is enormous. With his teacher's restraint, and sometimes virtual drabness, Telemann is much closer, for instance, to the classical Clementi, while Handel's melodic wealth and his glorious sublimity, sometimes almost pompous in its resplendence, might make him akin to the Romantic Weber. Or what will the teacher's opinion be, within one and the same "style", of the delicate sorrow that pervades Schubert's music and comes through even beneath the happiness, and is separated by a whole world from the Classical restraint or sparkling humour of the similarly "Romantic" Mendelssohn? And Beethoven's "style", perhaps the most extreme of all, where everything from outbursts of rage through painstaking craftsmanship to the most basic commonplaces can be found? And Mozart, the most polysemantic of the Classical masters? Clearly, such characteristics make a decisive impact on a performer when he commits himself to one master or another. And this is where teachers and performers fall into most of their errors, indeed, their greatest sins, when they set a seal on the composer's personal style—usually misinterpreting it as well—and then force it systematically on their pupils or their audience, filtered through their own obscurity. Perhaps Chopin is the most tragic victim of this *musical Procrustes' bed;* in teaching, and with the average performer, his music is characterized not by its brilliance but by overwhelming banality.

So what should the music teacher do? It is his duty to acquaint his pupils with style, as the composers' technique of a mode of expression. But beyond this he should not cite compulsory rules for the style of performance—there are no such things—only the artistic laws, which can be found in all good music.

VII TECHNIQUE

1 Its place in piano teaching

"The main issue is not the practice of technique but the technique of practice" (Liszt).

It is no accident that the chapter on technique has come in seventh place. The lessons of the previous six chapters were absolutely necessary if the element of piano-playing that makes music-making at all possible was to be put in a place worthy of it and rightfully its own.

These days, the view is generally accepted—even if it sometimes lacks the appropriate elucidation—that making music is the foremost objective, and manipulation of the instrument simply the indispensable means to that end. However virtuoso the performance may be, if it fails to support the music, it is worthless. Just what else besides technique is necessary if musical expression is to be effective the six previous chapters have endeavoured to explain, as they analysed the essence of the *object,* i.e. the *music,* and the characteristics of the *subject,* i.e. the *child,* in creative piano teaching, and went on to psychological and ethical influences and the role of style.

Why was this necessary?

A few quotations from Martienssen will help to justify it. "What is practised today under the banner of technique is not technique but mechanics. This distinction must be got across in piano teaching.... True virtuoso technique is when the technical apparatus has been thoroughly worked out from the inside outwards and is founded on creative demands in terms of sound. Anyone who thinks his talent comprises everything except technique is badly mistaken. Technique cannot be acquired separately but only together with demands in terms of sound.... If creative demands in terms of sound are the superior focal point for the player, then he will have a clear picture of what he wants to hear. *All the physical side of the playing apparatus has to do is to comply with this.* The connections between the two do not even come into his mind. Artistic achievement on the piano is only possible when the player's physical and mental being form a single psychophysical whole."

Of course the physical side of the playing apparatus can only comply in favourable circumstances. Clearly the technical conditions of instrumental playing are what make it possible for musical expression to become reality. Everyone knows this. But practising technique should not for a moment be divorced from musical volition (not even for finger exercises) and this is what teaching fails to take into account when it fixes technical objectives without the appropriate musical ideal, an ideal of sound. Countless books of method, studies, borrowed gimmicks, and more recently the results of scientific experiments, films and audio-visual tests have appeared over the years which deal with technique separately, disregarding musical concepts. The way to teach piano technique correctly ought not to be propounded independently of concrete musical tasks. Writing down, studying and slavishly copying detailed instructions and prohibitions in practice does not help much or result in any essential progress. In this matter, as in teaching generally, the rule applies that theoretically you can always learn from somebody (either what you should or what you should not do), but the true pedagogue will always take note of new data, critically filtering them through his own personality, so that, enriched by them, he can apply his own flexible method, according to the music, the pupil and the circumstances.

In view of this, an all-redeeming method for acquiring piano technique cannot be laid down. Many people have thought that by thorough systematization they have constructed a logical method that solves the question of correct piano-playing once and for all, whereas in fact they have simply put the finger on their own personal method, which was genuinely useful for them, and parts of which they or their successors were able to use with pupils of comparable temperament. In this way the various methodologies, often contradicting each other, were born, and the teachers who demanded that everyone should carry them out as universally valid, believing in good faith in the happiness of salvation.

Things like "the correct and universally valid teaching of technique", however, are quite impossible.

There are only two conceivable prerequisites for correct piano-playing, and without them nothing can be achieved in terms of movement:

a) balance in the position of the body, "from head to foot", and
b) well-exercised fingers.

2 The balance of the body

The first of these requirements is a prerequisite of all harmonious movement, and ought, in every sphere of life, from walking to movement on the highest artistic level, to have much greater attention paid to it. In some way or other, everyone is forced to create a balance between his organs of locomotion and the world about him, for otherwise his muscles would be incapable of accomplishing the most primitive of intended movements. The reason why babies keep snatching pointlessly at objects, and generally need a year and a half to learn how to walk, is because an enormous amount of experimenting and practice is necessary to achieve balance. The ability to make the correct movement depends on how far these experiments and exercises were to the point, or on whether carrying out the intended movement comes about in a state of harmonious balance. So *some* kind of balance arises in every movement; the question is, is this balance harmonious? When a child crouches at the piano and tries to make some sort of music on it for his own delight, without any guidance, he will also find the balance that it is easiest for him to attain. From the point of view of the aim to be achieved, however, this is not usually economical. The teacher must bring him round to a properly balanced position without destroying his inclination to go on "looking for" music.*

The prerequisite for harmonious movement is co-ordination in the working of opposing muscles and the ensuring of the time necessary for performing—executing—the movement. One of the major requirements here is for the playing apparatus to be relaxed.

But what do we mean by relaxed? If the whole playing apparatus were entirely relaxed—which does not take place perfectly even in a state of sleep—then there would be no muscular operation at all. The apparatus is called "relaxed" when the balance of the working of the muscles is correct, when the flexors and extensors—the opposing muscles—are working according to the tasks allotted to them. The opposite of this—stiffness—occurs when one group of muscles oversteps its function, and the other group of muscles, which is primarily responsible for the movement that has to be made, is compelled to accomplish its task in a forced manner. This is *the unproductive struggle between the muscles* that makes its appearance in cramped tenseness and stiff movements. Therefore the accurate way of describing the correct mechanism is not "relaxed" but "balanced".

The creation of balance in movement depends partly on physical and partly on psychological aptitudes. A capacity for physical dexterity can be inherited, so it is also a matter of talent; the effect the mind has on movement is at least as important a factor, and comes within teaching's sphere of influence. This links up with what I have referred to several times already—that the teacher's starting-point should be the child's spontaneous movement; he should not

---

*The teacher must learn to observe whether the back and shoulders are providing support, that is supply attuned to the deliberate movement of the fingers. "This is the one general external rule we would consider as binding. An excellent example of a state of spiritual and physical preparedness is given by the sitting position of Indian statues of Buddha. The stretching of the backbone at the sacrum and related sense of activity, as it seems, of the upper body propelling itself forward are the indispensable requirements, appropriate to every kind of adjustment, for the creation of interdependence between the body and the piano keyboard" (Martienssen). Perhaps the perfect harmony of movement in Hindu dancers and musicians is related to this ideal of balance.

provide patterns to be followed, as this hinders the development of the movement's individual balance.

In order therefore to avoid misunderstandings, let me set down the principle behind the teaching of movement: as the piano teaching progresses, occasional guidance in movement will be necessary to develop harmonious balance, but this should not occur according to a previously determined scheme considered to be universally valid, but by taking account of the child's personal physical and motoric functions, helping them on, gently correcting them, according to the dictates of musical conceptions and the demands in terms of sound.

3 The role of the fingers

The second requirement for correct piano-playing is well-exercised fingers. Properly speaking, this is tool-making, for it is the fingers that come into direct contact with the piano. This is why the acquisition of finger technique is the most time-consuming aspect of practice. Ever since the need for a written piano-teaching method has been apparent, the acquisition of finger technique has been the main aim. This naturally followed from the mechanism of the contemporary instruments, but endeavours that were directed exclusively to that end were also responsible for the greatest harm. Of course, it was not the discovery of the necessity for finger technique that was the error, but the more general phenomenon that pedagogical bureaucrats far removed from reality —from music—quickly lighted on the particular goal that they were capable of attaining within their limited horizons. Technical training for its own sake always stemmed from the fact that teachers lacking imagination found their pedagogical aims more easily here than in musical endeavours. The importance of developing finger-work was a correct discovery, only it became a curse, as a result of compulsory and over-emphatic bad teaching methods, firstly by crippling many hands, and secondly—once the over-emphasis was discovered —by leading to equally harmful reactions, such as the excesses of the so-called weight technique. The brilliant founders of the weight technique were in their turn followed by bureaucrats encapsulating everything into a rigid and infallible system, and only capable of conceiving of one kind of truth. The pedagogical bureaucrats split up into two fiercely warring factions, fanatically believing in either the finger or the weight technique as the sole means to salvation. (If neither theory is accepted as usable on its own, and if an explanation of the connection between the two is hardly necessary today, it is thanks to musician-teachers and performers with a concern for music.) These days, divisions of this sort into different technical types have to all intents and purposes come to an end. No one tries to teach technique without reference to the introduction of weight on the one hand, and finger activity, on the other. This was always the case for practising artists: the first-rate performers discovered the correct ratio with varying amounts of difficulty, while many players suffered as a result of rigid teaching methods.

Of course, what the fingers do occurs within the balance of the whole body. The teacher's intuition will determine the success of the training, according to his ability to see—and feel—what the matter is with the balance. Here, too, demands in terms of sound are the greatest help.

In connection with the fingers, the following should be observed:*
Touch itself consists of three stages:
A) preparation for the touch,
B) striking the key,
C) disengagement.

Stage A is the most important in terms of tone. This is where the correct conception has to appear that will exert the maximum influence on the tone. It is like the conductor's lead-in, which determines the tone, tempo, etc., of the orchestra. Or like the correct breath intake that is indispensable to a good voice. Or a more general example: before we can even say a word, we must be aware of the correct articulation for it. This is the secret of clear speaking. So preparation, the lead-in, plays a determining role in everything.

Stage B, as a function of the first, will only be correct if the pupil's fingers are capable of executing the conception mentioned above. The execution clearly depends on how well-exercised the fingers are. This is truly the most striking, most representative, most demonstrable, intelligible and audible aspect of touch. But it is not the only important one! It is very dangerous to deal with this alone. If the touch was not properly prepared in the first stage, it will be impossible to execute it correctly in the second. Pressing, snatching, the most common forms of trembling hands, inaudibility or a crude sound will be the result of starting the touch process with stage B. The same mistake occurs in miniature when a child "takes a dive" at the piano with no conception of the piece in question: he has hardly sat down before he is churning out what he has memorized.

It was for stage B, for the way the keys should be struck, that norms in teaching evolved most unambiguously, and as a result forced the most compulsory rules on the methodologies. Among the strictest rules in the last century and at the beginning of this were:

---

*Generally, of course, there is no need to bring this to the knowledge of the pupils in this form; a pupil with demands in terms of sound will find the solution spontaneously, and a pupil without them cannot be "persuaded" by being made aware of the theory, but by having his overall demands in terms of sound developed.

a) striking the keys with raised fingers, to encourage their independence;
b) a dropped wrist, to make raising the fingers easier;
c) this was linked with the form of practice whereby, with one finger held strictly down, the other fingers increased their independence by being raised high before striking the keys;
d) severely retracted fingers, so that the keys would be struck hammer-like by the finger-tips.

All the exercises in this connection served to strengthen the fingers' freedom from each other, and accordingly dealt only with dynamics, having nothing to do with tonal colour. Finger exercises entirely filled the first weeks of learning, with music being dealt with in theoretical form only; the sole aim was to make the fingers adept at striking the keys. The sequence of events was therefore: first exercise the fingers mechanically, without music, and then have a try at striking the keys while producing some sort of musical fragment. (We might recall the child-prodigy situation as the converse of this music-free process.) Such were the norms of the second stage of the touch. Sadly, they still exist, if in a more attractive form, today. And if, generally speaking, learning to play the piano begins with learning music in the sense that it deals with living music—folksong—even present-day practice concentrates on the norms of touch rather than on the sound, and though it starts with melodies and not finger exercises, it still places the greater emphasis on the touch and not the sound. Even according to today's norms making the fingers stronger and more independent occupies the foremost place. Fundamentally this would be all right, but only in conjunction with musical requirements and in their service. The purpose of strengthening the fingers and making them work independently is not to make them strong and free of each other; the note, the melody must be attended to, having first been pre-conceived and subsequently checked to see if it came out in the second stage of the touch.

Attention should not be on the movement, but on the sound, to which the movement should be adjusted! But in that case there are no predetermined norms, since every child will strive for the best sound according to his own conception. First and foremost he will listen, trying to bring into being the ideal sound. *This* is where the teacher can then help him, according to the way the child's physique—his hands—are personally best suited to the touch and the sound. The difference in the order of events is enormous, isn't it?

But even here there are norms, of course. Clearly, the ideal sound cannot be brought into being with splayed or cramped hands, etc. We should, however, derive the norms from the music, from listening, rather than figure out the music from the movement.

Exercising the fingers depends primarily not on strengthening the finger-muscles but on developing a delicate sense of touch. Developed finger-muscles and more nimble fingers will not be obtained exclusively by strengthening the muscles. According to Martienssen: "The strength of fingers is their speed". That is: the individual finger strikes decisively and roundedly not by using all its strength but by playing easily and energetically, with the dynamically working muscles. We cannot rely too much on the fingers' strength, partly because to exert strength is not the function of finger-muscles—that is left to larger organs in the production of the sound—and partly because the true function of the fingers—agility—should be developed, and not the exertion of strength. To some extent the two things are mutually exclusive; the exertion of strength inhibits agility. A good finger technique cannot be ponderous. Striking certain notes weightily, below a certain tempo, comes, of course, under another category. But in teaching beginners, however, allowance must be made here, too, for what the hand and fingers, can stand. If a pupil's dynamic range is greater than what his fingers are capable of, he will help things along with caved-in fingers and trembling hands. When teaching starts, these pupils with weak joints but strong personalities present the teacher with a difficult choice. The above-mentioned faults figure as mortal sins in teaching. But from the point of view of the future the danger is even greater if the pupils with weak hands are protected from caved-in fingers and trembling hands by using an excessively gentle touch. They will, at the same time, become habituated to a colourless, dull, overcautious and characterless sound from which their tonal range will hardly progress at all. This inaudibility may have its humane side with respect to neighbours and noise disturbance, but it blocks off the path to lively and colourful playing, and the tonal range will find it more difficult to re-emerge later on. We should not forget that we should feel the keys and the instrument not just with our fingers, but with our whole bodies, and if we are overcautious this becomes impossible. If a child has to take care over too many things, he loses confidence, and will find it difficult to re-discover the impetus he had to start with. Most children—particularly the most talented ones—cannot tolerate restrictions like this, and lose interest in playing the piano at the very beginning of their studies. Insisting on colourless, overcautious piano-playing has already caused a good deal of dropping out.

On the other hand, however, we must keep an eye on the other extreme. The overcautious, colourless and insipid sound in fashion today came about in the wake of the badly interpreted weight technique.

There are fingers that are naturally endowed with strong muscles, and whose joints are resistant. Fingers blessed with joints of this kind do not cave in, for they support the weight put upon them—given the necessary position—through the natural strength of the fingers. For children like this, we can successfully call for the rounded, arched positioning of the fingers, since the muscles and joints feel where the balance is produced. But if the joints are weak, explaining the positioning of the fingers does not help much, because the joints can only bear the lightest of loads. Gradually, however, the weaker joints in the fingers grow stronger, and by keeping alive the tonal demands and developing the sense of touch, caving-in and trembling can be cured more easily than an overcautious and colourless sound.

In fact piano-playing can be begun with extended fingers, if the pupil can play the note better that way; with time, if we point out that he should feel the keys on the tips of his fingers, he will retract his fingers himself, in so far as this suits the form of his hand. But it is important for him, as he touches the keys, to feel the five keys beneath his five fingers. After a short time he will also sense the five-finger position when his fingers are not touching the keys. Finger technique cannot be acquired with fingers that are always resting on the keys. The pupil must arrive at a point where he feels the same position not only from the surface of the keys but also at a certain distance. How this is developed is a completely individual matter. There are children who immediately sense the stable position over a range of five keys, and there are others who are constantly shifting their fingers about. It should be noted that the latter are generally the more dexterous and nimble, but it is very difficult to get them used to even a minimal amount of stableness—yet this is indispensable, even with the freest forms of movement. So it is a question of balance between stability and agility. Movement, like the musical process, at times requires nimbleness and variety, at times premeditated stability and patience.

Stage C—that after striking the key, the finger that has completed its task should relax in the appropriate manner—will occur correctly if the pupil directs his attention towards the first stage of the next note. For the beginning can only be good when the end that preceded it was meaningful. Then the key will push back the relaxed finger with its own force.

4 Ways of striking the keys

Something must be said here about ways of striking the keys; for although the answers to such matters belong rather to the sphere of sonority, they are usually ranked among questions of the way technique is taught. It is not my intention to analyse the technical solutions to the problems of striking the keys, for that would be falling into my own trap. But the teacher should know about the different kinds of touch, which express different kinds of sound, and should teach them accordingly by stimulating the pupil's sense of sonority. As I have stated: if the pupil has a clear picture of what he wants to hear, then the only matter for the playing apparatus is to fit in with these demands. Without trying to be all-embracing, we should sort out the various types of touch. Not the way they are achieved, but requirements in sound that result from ways of striking the keys. Once more a clarification of terminology is of primary importance.

The way a piano piece is to be performed is usually indicated to a greater or lesser extent by the composer. Of course, when the composer writes staccato, portato, etc. in the score, he is thinking of the sound, and not of the touch. Unfortunately, piano teaching has generally treated these indications as instructions on touch (even if not meant as such by the composer), and written rules have come into being on the appropriate ways of striking the keys. Yet like every other musical expression, the markings used by composers cannot be explained in one way alone. A hundred different types of staccato, legato, portato, leggiero, etc. are possible, according to the mood and character of the music. Such expressions are usually taught as ways of striking the keys, which as such would not be a problem (indeed it is natural that the physical means to producing a sound should preoccupy the teacher), if the way in which the motoric execution is to be brought about did not conceal the composer's instruction concerning the sound. Let me illustrate the difference with a distressingly concrete example: it is observable that whenever a piece is played before an audience of experts they always devote much more attention to the *spectacle* presented by the pupil's piano-playing than to the *sound,* which is thus most often not the purpose of this touch but simply the consequence of it. Of course, it is simpler to examine and pass judgement with one's eyes than with one's ears. (As if we were not dealing with music teachers.) That the staccato was not supple and the tenuto did not come from the arm—everyone could see that; but did everyone hear whether it sounded the way the music demanded? And even if they do hear, they still mostly criticize pupil and teacher on the movement rather than the sound. There is no time left to discuss the sound. In this way musical markings are taught as touch markings by the teacher, who judges them accordingly at test time. It is unlikely that this meets with the approval of the composer.

5 Fingering

The question of fingering is a particularly complicated part of piano teaching. Here again the principle mentioned above can be repeated: there can be no single universal rule for fingering. Perhaps the only rule when teaching beginners is that they must be made to feel the position of five fingers to five keys during the first weeks; this, perhaps, is what must be demanded almost mercilessly. The five finger spread is the pianist's yardstick—being sure of it, he can work out the other positions. This makes it possible for the pupil, right at the beginning of his studies, to play pieces ranging over a pentachord with his eyes constantly following the score, for his fingers will feel which key is coming next. If he plays tunes from a score that can be picked out in the five-finger spread, he should not be allowed to look at his hand. This is the prerequisite of early and confident playing from the score. This is difficult to put into practice with beginners with an exceptionally good ear, as they are inclined to feel by ear for tunes they partly know, and use every means they can to get round the difficult art of score-reading. We should allow them to play a lot by ear as well, but accurate playing from the score must be constantly and rationally practised with them.

6 The teacher's physical involvement

It has been mentioned several times already that in planning movement in detail, that is, in guiding his pupil's movements, a teacher must pay very great attention to the pupil's inborn movements or those he produces which have become habitual in everyday life. Present in the teacher's mind must be the movement that works most to the pupil's advantage. Not the movement that seems the most obvious to the teacher—bearing in mind the one ultimately aimed at—but the one that is most suitable for the pupil at a given moment. This, however, can only be achieved by the teacher who, in the course of attentive teaching and of his own piano practice, has acquired, over a shorter or longer period, the capacity for "ideomotoric introjection" (Martienssen). This means that rather than endeavouring to implant his own mechanism into his pupil, the teacher tries to enter into the pupil's state of being. By observing the child's movements and way of thinking, he tries to adopt his muscular attitude. If I cannot feel something in my own muscles, then how can I correct the way they function? The capacity for ideomotoric introjection can be found in the work of every true-born teacher. One can still be a musical, inspiring, first-rate music teacher without it, but the lack of the ability to identify can be the cause of many errors.

Fortunately, even those who did not spontaneously acquire a mastery of it by inclination, the capacity for ideomotoric introjection can be acquired, through great concentration and application, provided they respect the dialectics of teaching and everything that pertains to it. But we should not make a fetish of this ability. If it is basically dictated by movement rather than sound, it will not be worth a penny.

VIII PROFESSIONAL TRAINING AND MASS EDUCATION

1 The diversity of music

For several pages in the fourth chapter I attempted to demonstrate that every kind of musical activity flows from the same source, and that in musical evaluation there is no fundamental difference between productive and reproductive artists, aestheticians, and the most disparate types of amateurs. As the main proof I used the thesis that music's content is the way the music is shaped. It is the shaping that produces the masterpiece, and it is the way the shaping is done that is the common factor for the composer, the performer, the analyser and the music lover, and makes us all respond in harmony. Everyone, therefore, however they are involved with music, belongs to one family. This much is clear. And the whole of humanity could be members of this family.

The musical instinct is not the privilege of the elect. Everyone who was not born deaf has it—for music developed from hearing.

Everyone who is not blind looks, and everyone who is not deaf listens, but how few actually see and hear! "Homo sapiens": i.e. everyone thinks in some form or other: yet how few really have perception. Kodály's slogan "music belongs to everybody" is fine. But it is only a partial expression of the thesis that humanity should be one great family. Kodály had a Christ-like conception of how this great musical family was to be brought about. But he provided only theoretical aspects towards the elaboration of a practical method. He wanted to translate his theory into practice with all his persistence, energy, competence and wisdom. What he saw as the culmination of this theory was his desire for a "singing Hungary". But music is not only singing; a person may be able to sing or even solmizate with great virtuosity and yet be no musician; another may not be able to sing, but music is still for him. Music has very many aspects, and in its infinite variety it can come to belong to more and more members of the human race.

But how can music be for everybody?

I shall try to throw some light on the matter by quoting an old sarcastic anecdote, which said: anyone who is no good at playing the violin can still become a viola-player; if he's not dexterous enough for the viola either, he can go to the front of the orchestra and be the conductor; and if he's not even suitable for that, he can always be a musicologist. If we take the anecdote lightheartedly, there is a lot more wisdom in it than sarcasm. It really means that music has such a broad and expensive domain that anyone with some sort of

capacity for it will undoubtedly find a place there somewhere. Two conditions are necessary here:
  a) the person in question should be genuinely musical,
  b) he should look for his position in the right place.

Those whose physical attributes are a hindrance should not try to compete with aspiring virtuosi; if they do not have sufficient wealth of invention, they should not try to become composers, and so on. Provided they do not cling stubbornly to a single obsession, they will be able to do many things that significantly promote musical culture, and link up with the great family. Every branch is in great need of suitable talent, but has no need at all of things forced on it insincerely from the outside.

"Music belongs to everybody."

When Kodály spoke of musical culture, he always thought of singing. His ideal was the Italian madrigal school. This inspired his working activity through many decades, and this is where he achieved his results of world-wide significance. "Hungary's reputation in the world" can be put down to this. This is how Kodály laid the foundations. He had only one demand as far as instrumental teaching was concerned: that it, too, should be music. It must be admitted, this is a very modest and very general requirement, and can be easily misinterpreted. And it has, indeed, been misinterpreted, both well-meaningly and maliciously, with professional and amateurish zeal. Instrumental teaching has not always fittingly translated Kodály's far-reaching wisdom into its own language, and is not always justified in partaking of its glory. As far as the financial requirements of "music belongs to everybody" are concerned, those of instrumental teaching came off even worse than the average. But as we have said, the slogan itself did not sufficiently inspire instrumental teaching and those in charge of it. Perhaps they did not even adopt it, for it was only natural that they were dealing solely with people who already wanted to make music their own.

But does music belong to everyone who goes in for it?

This is where the great clash occurred between the profession and the mass-movement, in respect of singing and music on the one hand, and instrumental specialist and mass teaching on the other.

2 Reform and revolution

Reforms and revolutions have occurred several times in the history of music teaching concurrently with the evolution of instruments and with changes in social conditions.

What is the real difference between reform and revolution?

Reforms tend to take place at times when it has become obvious that certain outdated features and distortions are visible in teaching methods, and these must be carefully replaced, or improved, and set in order. Revolution by contrast dynamically brushes away what is outworn and false and essentially contributes something decisively different towards development.

There is a concept whereby change is a step forward by comparison with the past, even if it is based on faulty premises. Even change on the wrong track promotes development, at least by bringing the old into question, and may perhaps through its very mistakes help to substantiate what in the old was good and had proved of lasting value. What today seems an enormous achievement, however, may become out of date tomorrow, and an obstacle to development. Revolution is a struggle where forces clash, and out of the clash comes a balance. Reform is the opposite of this. Its vocation is to restrain, control and order the achievements—perhaps already outdated—of the revolution. Revolution is movement, reform is careful systematization. Revolution breaks out through impatience at what is old; reform is born of a sober mind.

In Hungary, after the liberation in 1945, a music teaching revolution broke out. It was prepared for by the movement carried on before the outbreak of the Second World War by the Hungarian Chorus, under Kodály's guidance, and entitled Singing Youth. Progressive instrumental teachers also wanted to take part in this movement, for they saw that the bases of Hungarian music-teaching methods also needed to be created anew in the same way as school singing teaching, and all the more so since Hungarian piano teaching had been at a low level for decades. (I shall not deal with those isolated phenomena, the circle of brilliant music teachers and the innovators grouped around them, whose work made more of a stir abroad, since its originators and followers were "personae non gratae" for the government of the time.)

The watchword of the movement that began after the liberation was: the material for music teaching should also be based on the folksong, i.e., learning an instrument should begin with music.

The vocal and instrumental revolution, like every healthy ambition at that time, aimed at raising the musical level of the masses. The school-choir culture and the chorus movement itself did not look for the answer in teaching methods but in teaching materials, so that the material itself would then determine the changes in method. The movement's leaders were wise enough to know that this is the right way. Solmisation did not produce the folksong-cult in Hungary; the cult of good music produced the "Kodály Method".

With folksong as the beginning, the old unmusical finger exercises became untenable on the piano, too. And in this way the instrumental revolution came about—sweeping away the old-fashioned methods along with the unmusical material.

It is not our concern to look into the further development of the choral culture; we are following the path traced by the piano-teaching revolution. Here, along with unquestionable revolutionary achievements, mistakes were also made on several occasions, and constantly posed a threat—and still do—through their retrogressive power.

The great deficiency of the piano-teaching revolution of 1945 was that there was not time to clarify the new concepts that had burst on the scene. The new doctrines sprang up with such an elemental force that they surprised everyone who had a spark of the urge to develop within him. There was a revolution.

Its foremost goal was mass teaching, and primarily a radical change in teaching for beginners. This could not have been otherwise: the foundations had to be laid. The way the movement's fervent adherents persevered and sacrificed themselves was unparalleled and impressive, but it lacked a precise overall perspective and refined discrimination. The standard-bearers were mainly the teachers of beginners, and their organizers were not blessed with such prophetic faculties that they could have foreseen the dangers that stem from this. Those obsessed with mass education did not realize that laying the foundations of musical culture did not depend only on teaching the masses. The starting-point was correct, for here was the greatest need, but along with mass teaching, the "musical elite", at least in the long term, should have been considered. Plans should have been laid straight away, in the heat of the revolution, from kindergarten to academy, with Kodály-like wisdom. Today we can see that this did not happen, and we can also see how much this has endangered, and still endangers, the straight line of development. What we cannot know is whether a distinction could have been made there and then under the enchantment of the mass movement. Might not prudent foresight have slowed down the dynamism of the revolution too much? There was still a lot we did not know, and that could only have come to light later; for example, we were not acquainted with the child-prodigy syndrome discovered by Martienssen, or with many other things that we could only have hit upon later, after we had understood that music had to be studied much more thoroughly if the revolutionary achievements were to come to perfection.

Professional training and mass education? The education of amateurs, professionals and passive culture-carriers? Reconciling these things and segregating them still remains to be done, and cannot be put off, for the confusion is endangering development more and more.

The whole world is in a state of perpetual motion; those who do not move forwards slip back, for there is no stopping. How could teaching be the exception, when it is primarily one of life's moving forces, even if it is sometimes compelled to be a restraining influence? The teaching of music must find its bearings in the light of what I have said above.

In the finger-exercise conscious world before the revolution, everyone's fingers were trained, even if there was not the remotest hope that they would ever be able to put them to good use. If they could not then they should not play the piano. During the revolution, everyone had to sing, and it was practically a crime if they happened to move their fingers. The crucial thing was hearing the music, *without motoric help*. What is wrong if the two things help each other? Indeed, is it permissible to put the question: either fingers alone, or music alone?

And what about the child, who would perhaps have preferred using his fingers at the piano to singing? Admittedly the throat is the cheapest and most accessible instrument but what if someone has no use for it? The type of instrument was virtually born with the child. Can we be allowed to interfere? It is just as arbitrary to distract attention from instrumental music through non-instrumental music as it is a crime to destroy a child's delight in music by forcing instrumental manipulative skills on him. One child will become interested in music one way, another the other, and with the right person a love of music can be inculcated not only through folksongs and Mozart, but even through Czerny, too. One thing is certain: movement divorced from hearing together with theory cannot, either in the beginning or later, be a foundation for music; the foundation can only be sincere music tailored to the pupil's personality.

3 Making a choice

We had arrived at the idea that within music's many-sided domain the teacher should find the appropriate place for his pupil in the great family. It must be emphasized, however, that it is not true that everyone can be taught music. It is generally considered in child psychology that to all intents and purposes the bases of a child's education are laid by the time he is two. Before then, and still more so afterwards, so many different influences can impinge on the child, affecting his attitude to music, that all we can say is: *almost* every child can be taught music. Teaching theory does not have to reckon with the tiny proportion of unteachables; it will emerge in the course of learning that we are dealing with exceptional cases—rejects. I thought it important to point this out simply so that teachers should not be tense and anxious in their work if there is one child they cannot get along with, even though to the best of their knowledge they have done everything possible. There are unteachable children, and not all of them are unmusical. But as I have said, this observation merely serves to reassure the teacher; in theory the proportion is negligible.

We need to discover in which direction to guide the child, and where his aptitudes lead him. There must be no mistake, it is not a question of what he feels like doing, but of what he is apt for. The difference is enormous. It is a very common phenomenon for a child to want to do one thing or another because he feels that it is his weak point, and he would like to prove the opposite. It is very common, for instance, for those whose movements are awkward to want to be virtuosi, and so on. Guidance must be very cautious and well considered, in order to avoid dissuading the child from one branch and yet not putting anything in its place. If the pupil is musical, the teacher must find and develop the child's liking for the field where he will best be able to exercise his abilities. This also means that the teacher must not be biassed against any one field, and must guide his pupil according to the latter's abilities and his own *knowledge*, and not his own taste.

The main task during the early years is to find out what type the child belongs to. Virtually everyone can be useful in some capacity in the field of music, it is a matter of finding where. A good teacher can extract the maximum from every child, but all "results" that are forcibly drummed into him are worthless. One must know the music, know the pupil, and work towards and co-ordinate the essence of each.

4 Streaming

There is much argument on whether, and when, pupils suitable for a career in music should be separated from those who will be amateurs. It is indisputable that children of varying ability cannot be taught lumped together. The slower development of those with less ability has a worse effect on the more talented ones than does the latter's better development on the former. Comparison between pupils is also a very doubtful weapon. It is wrong for them to measure their development against each other; it should be measured against music. They should keep their attention on music and not on each other. Up till now, the division into streams "A" and "B" has been the most practicable, though even here we cannot boast of much success. But the reason for this is the fixed class and teaching material. The class for exceptional talents instituted at the Academy of Music in Budapest is another possible solution. Within these divisions almost everything could be resolved, but only on the basis of moral principles. This, sadly, is still on a fairly weak footing today. In Chapter V I dealt separately with the ethics of music teaching. Here I should perhaps raise one or two aspects that are a hindrance to the evolution of the family of music.

Today, the evaluation of talent from kindergarten to college suffers from a certain fixation on the concert platform. It is my contention that the origins of this derive not from the child but from the ineradicable vanity of teachers and parents. This is what largely determines teaching today. Even a talent that genuinely identifies with music is infected by this pedagogical attitude, which forces the pupil into considering that sooner or later the platform, and applause, and success, will be more important to him than music. This also does a lot of harm to the less gifted, whom it compels to use the small amount of time left to them to learn in preparation for demonstration and joint classes, examinations and concerts.

The question arises here as in many other places: what are we hurrying for? How can we go deeply into anything when we are rushing so much? Another factor is that music schools do not have a good working relationship with general schools. Music schools cannot compete with these schools in terms of method and a precise order of events. The connection between school and learning music cannot mean that they are one and the same thing. Within the music school itself, music teaching remains individual teaching, even in group classes. Rivalry is a very two-edged weapon, goading rather than inspiring. The laws that govern schools can do a lot of harm to music teaching, for even within a state framework, music teaching must remain strictly individual.

It seems that for the time being no better solution presents itself where the individual nature of teaching could be better ensured than the "A" and "B" streams, and the creation of the Academy's class for exceptional talent. There would, however, be ways of using these better in order to get nearer the great musical family. Ways, but not a method! On the contrary, less method is needed. More time and freedom should be given in music teaching to both the teacher and the pupil. The teacher should not be bound by restrictions on classes and teaching materials, nor the pupil by prescribed patterns. The greater the opportunity for free choice, and the fewer "shoulds" and "musts", the more opportunities there will be for getting to know the types of pupil and making more use of variety. Music teaching today is *based on mistrust*. The obligations imposed are proof of this. The teaching material prescribed for every class must be completed with the appropriate technique, teaching must be carried out in the prescribed manner, and so on. Yet the more freedom is given in teaching, the more innovations and variations come into being. The teacher's personal responsibility, which is worth more than any supervision, comes into full play, and the type and quality of the talent comes all the more reliably to light. Of course, more time and inventiveness is needed for this than for ticking off the specified procedures. Teacher training and beginner teachers should be emancipated; more personal responsibility should be demanded of them and less dutiful obedience. They will then be more likely to be able to pass this on, so that the personal responsibility in learning music will find fuller expression in the pupils, too. There should be more time and freedom for the teacher to discover which musical type the pupil belongs to. There should be more time for the pupil himself to try out a variety of things during the lesson, and to find—under the teacher's patient guidance—the one that suits him best. It is not a question of making the lessons longer, for a child's average ability to concentrate hardly goes beyond 40–50 minutes. But this time should be less restricted, more varied, more personal—more interesting.

5 Auxiliary subjects

This is the term I would use for all the musical occupations that are not directly connected with the instrument—preparatory courses, solfeggio, theory, musical appreciation. A lot has been said already about preparatory courses. I think their tasks and methods are fairly settled and by and large they fulfil their function.

Officially there were auxiliary subjects in old-style music teaching too. But as teaching generally went on privately and virtually without supervision, they were almost—or completely—sabotaged. They were clearly considered superfluous. They entailed additional expense for private music schools, and unpleasant extra work for the pupils. We must admit that apart from the Academy of Music, where for the most part the auxiliary subjects were taught by musicians of great learning, who were convinced of their importance and taught them in such a way as to convince their students as well, the subsidiary subjects have never been popular, not even after they were designated with the title of "compulsory" in order to increase their standing. And justly so. Generally, these subjects served to make the students swot up the dull theoretical knowledge related to learning an instrument. Accordingly it was known as musicology.

Here, too, the music-teaching revolution brought about a radical change: singing and musical dictation based on folk music became the exclusive material for solfeggio. To begin with, this subject was treated fairly loosely; there was no prescribed teaching material and still less methodology. Accordingly, those teachers who had a good instinct for music and teaching did it well, i.e. musically more profitably; the poorer teachers did it to less musical advantage, but on the whole as a pleasant game. Although not everyone saw the sense of it, solfeggio was at any rate a game that dealt with music. Those who understood what it was about were able to use it to develop the ear and a feeling for music.

This state of idyllic freedom was wrecked not by the children or the parents but by the instrumental teachers, who begrudged solfeggio its one hour a week. The need arose for the tasks and objectives of solfeggio to be determined in the same way as the material of instrumental study had been precisely laid down like a school course. Unfortunately, when the auxiliary subjects were decided upon, the "help" took on a meaning that was much nearer the old musicology than the ideal conceived by Kodály, according to which it was solfeggio's concern to supply the musical development sometimes missing from instrumental study with solmization and musical dictation. This alone was not an effective way of making instrumental teaching musical. But it was better than nothing.

It is now common knowledge—even if the efforts accompanying it are not always successful—that instrumental teaching must be based on musical foundations, for solfeggio cannot alone make up its musical deficiencies. Above and beyond the instrument, we must penetrate to the essence of music, and this penetration must be helped by the auxiliary subjects, based mainly not on instrumental but other activities and theory. It is not the task of the auxiliary subjects, as in times past, to relieve the music teacher of the disagreeable and boring side of teaching, like score-reading, the study of scales and intervals, etc., but to approach music from an aspect different from that of the instrument teacher. Thus the auxiliary subjects should be in the service of music, and not of the instrument teacher.

Their methods should, however, vary, and a more thorough and profound study is to be expected from musicians-to-be in both the technical and the theoretical fields, while the members of music's more extensive family can easily be spared both regular practice of technique and a knowledge of the scientific bases of music.